SECRETS OF THE INCAS

A MODERN APPROACH TO ANCIENT RITUAL AND PRACTICE

By
Michael Peter Langevin

NEW PAGE BOOKS
A Division of The Career Press, Inc.
Franklin Lakes, NJ

Secrets of the Ancient Incas
Edited by Dee Josephson
Typeset byDM Cradle Associates
Cover design by Diane Y. Chin
Printed in the U.S.A. by Book-mart Press

To order this title, please call toll-free 1-800-CAREER-1 (NJ and Canada: 201-848-0310) to order using VISA or MasterCard, or for further information on books from Career Press.

The Career Press, Inc., 3 Tice Road, PO Box 687,
Franklin Lakes, NJ 07417
www.careerpress.com
www.newpagebooks.com

Library of Congress Cataloging-in-Publication Data

Langevin, Michael Peter, 1952-
    Secrets of the ancient Incas : a modern approach to ancient ritual and practice / by
    Michael Peter Langevin
        p. cm.
    Includes bibliographical references (p.) and index.
    ISBN 1-5641j4-602-2 (paper)
        1. Shamanism—Peru. 2. Incas—Religion—Miscellanea. 3. Spiritual life—
    Miscellanea. 4. Inc I. Title.

    BF1622.14 L36 2002
    299'.88323—dc21
2002022228

Dedication

I dedicate this book:

To my strong wife Deborah Lynn Genito who keeps me grounded and makes my life meaningful.

To Sophia Zila Langevin—the best daughter a man could ever ask for whose laughter and insights always bring me great joy.

To Henry Miguel Langevin—the best son a man could ever ask for, whose intensity and persistence inspire me.

To Eileen Winifred Gibbons, my mom—her unconditional love and nature walks with me as a kid have given me my foundation for life.

To Louis Lloyd Langevin, my dad, and his wife Gemma Langevin—their friendship and great attitudes in these recent decades inspire me and help me to live in health and with optimism.

To Spider, Pat, Nancy, Liz, Dan, and Susanne—a man is only an outgrowth of what his siblings help him to become. I love them all dearly and am blessed to have shared their love all my life. There is no love as deep and unqualified as a family's.

To Rueben, Freea, and Ayla Langevin—to be a godfather is an honor that is a challenge to live up to but also a sharing that is like no other relationship in life.

To Bill and Rose Genito for being great In-laws and grand parents
To Sirona Knight, Mike Starwind, and Skylar who set a fine example and helped make this book happen.

To the Famila Wells, Tim, Betty, Mila, and Joaquin— they gave us Cusco and the Sacred Valley.

To Nielda, Paulito Callanaupa, and their sons for their great work.

To Lottie Hacket, David Himmer, and Richard Dabb—true friends all.

To everyone who ever worked with Magical Blend and MB Media, especially Tracy, René, Susan, and Deanna.

To the Peruvian and Andean people of today-how can a people be so loving and embracing? Thank you all. I know your future is bright.

To my agent, Lisa Hagen and to Mike Lewis who believed in this project and was were to give it a chance.

To my friend and editor Mike Richman who made it much smoother.

And to the Inca Gods and Goddess. They have become friends and advisors. This book is only part of our deal!

Contents

Introduction **9**
Meeting the Incan Gods 9
Why Peru? 10
The Journey 11
Machu Picchu 12
The Gods 14
The Initiation 21
The Compromise 23

1 *Who Were the Incas?* **27**
How Old Is the Incan Culture? 28
The Territory 29
The Myths 31
The Sapa Incas 32
The Religious Beliefs 35
The Religious Offices 36
A Citizen's Life 38
The People's Spirituality 42

2 *Becoming a Family* **45**
Commitment 46
Peru 48
The Joining 49
The Process 50
The Return 52

3 *Living the Incan Life* **55**
Focusing Your Intent and Realigning
    Your Vision 56

Finding a Nature Spirit Guide   62
The Power of Nature Spirits   64
Emotional Energies   65
Finding Allies   67
Accessing Other Dimensions   70
Adaptability   72

4 *Thinking of the Incas* **75**
Visualization and Goal Setting   76
America and Peru   78
A Rainy Night in Cusco   79

5 *Incan Rituals* **81**
Background of Incan Rituals   82
Magical Rituals   87
Creating a Reservoir for Your Magical
   Energies   88
Passing Down the Traditions
   of Shamanic Energies   89
Rites of Initiation   90
Shamanic Initiation Rituals   91
Gathering Incan Ceremonial Tools   93
Incan Ceremonial Tools   94
Incan Ceremonial Tools Explained   96
My First Magical Staff   102
The Proper Energies   103

6 *Further Incan Ritual* **107**
Chinchero   108
Assuming the Energy of the Gods
   and Goddesses   109
The Incan Pantheon   110
Invoking Pacsa Mama and the Energies
   of the Moon Goddess   114
Death and the Dead as Allies   116
Offering of the Essence   118
Home Blessing   118

Requesting Favors from the Gods
and Goddesses   120

7   *Pisac* **125**
Ruins   126
A Night on the Town   129
The Morning After   131

8   *Incan Dreaming* **133**
An Overview of Incan Dreaming   134
Dreaming of a Different Reality   136
Ayahuasca and San Pedro   138
Physical Applications   1410
Dreaming With a Goal in Mind   143

9   *Puno, Bolivia, and Tiwanaku* **145**
Puno   145
Copacabana   149
La Paz   151
Tiwanaku   155
Back to Cusco   159

10   *Incan Creativity* **161**
Incan and Peruvian Creativity   163
Music   164
Literature   166
Dance   167
Weaving the Textures of Our Lives   169
Andean Landscape Art   171
The Other Arts   173
Cultivating Incan Creativity   174

11   *Incan Living—The Archetypical Inca Trail* **179**
Attitude of the Incas   180
The Inca Trail   181
Suggestions for Beginning to Climb
the Archetypical Inca Trail   183

12 *Summing It Up—Epilogue* *189*
Now and Then   190

Glossary *195*

Bibliography *201*

Index *205*

Introduction

Meeting the Incan Gods

Three decades ago, the Incan Gods and Goddesses assigned a mission to a frightened 21-year-old from Methuen, Massachusetts. That young man was me. The book that you now hold in your hands is the fulfillment of one part of the promise that I made to those Gods and Goddesses on that day, in a dark cave outside the holy site of Machu Picchu in Peru. It is a mission that has helped to shape and define my adult life.

It is now the year 2002, and I am again visiting Peru in search of my destiny. This time I am here with my wife Deborah and my children Henry and Sophia. All of us have spent these last four months exploring the people and lands of Peru, and the cultures and traditions of the Incan people. It is particularly gratifying for me to see the growth of my children in this, the land of their birth. That's another part of the story, and another part of my promise to the Gods.

This book is an outgrowth of my experiences and research into the culture and practices of the ancient and modern Incan people. It contains numerous rites and rituals that have been used by the Incas for thousands of years; they are still in widespread use today. These practices are timeless, and these techniques work! You can employ them in your own life, just as they appear here, or you can adapt them in ways that best fit you and your belief system. It is inevitable that everyone will respond differently to this information, because we have all taken different roads to this one singularity of time called the present. My own path was tangled and twisted up in the history of Peru and the overpowering commands of the Incan Gods and Goddesses. Travel with me back through time to share my first meeting in this life with the Incan Gods and Goddesses.

In the fall of 1973, I was a junior in college in Boston. My greatest hero in those days was Che Guevera, a man who had dedicated his life to helping the poor people of the world fulfill their potential. I had decided to major in Latin American studies, with the goal of either becoming a revolutionary or a guerilla diplomat bent on changing the way that the United States government dealt with Latin American nations.

Why Peru?

That semester, I had a wonderful teacher who had spent the previous summer traveling throughout Latin America. The country that really stole her heart was Peru. As I would later discover for myself, the Peruvian people are very loving. The ruins of their ancestral settlements are awe-inspiring and other-worldly, and the Andes are uniquely majestic. Peru was also one of the few Latin American countries to experience a leftist military *coup d'état* in which the officers were really committed to land reform, improved education, and a better life for the poor.

The class that I took that semester could have been renamed "The Spell of the Incas." By December first, I knew that I needed to see Peru at once. At the time, I was working nights as a waiter at a hip Cambridge restaurant named the Turtle Cafe. I generally waited on Harvard professors and students in my trademark derby hat. The job enabled me to save a little bit of money, which stretched even further once I stopped purchasing food. I lived on just one meal a day—dinner. I ate just before beginning my shift at the Turtle Cafe. Both of these things—the small amount of cash as well as my body's acclimation to a reduced caloric intake—would help me greatly in the trials to come.

The Journey

Immediately after finals, I bought early Christmas presents for my family and friends. Then, on a snowy early morning, I took off hitch-hiking south from Boston since I couldn't afford airfare directly to Peru. I could (just barely) afford it from Miami, so off I went down the eastern seaboard. The hitch down was very long and very cold, and I ate little for the next few weeks. Finally arriving at the Miami airport, I purchased my ticket for Lima, which left me with less than $60 to cover expenses while in Peru. I didn't plan to eat much, and I figured that I could sleep outdoors. So off I flew on Aero Peru.

I landed at the Lima airport about four in the afternoon. After obtaining directions to downtown Lima, I strapped on my backpack and began walking. It was warm and the airport is far from Lima proper. After hiking for about an hour, a truck pulled over and the driver asked me where I was headed.

When I told him in my terrible Spanish, he began to laugh. He asked where I was staying, and I replied that I wasn't sure. He laughed once again and invited me to dinner. What luck! The man lived in a small barrio on the outskirts of town. The local priest's English was better than my Spanish, so he sat with us, drinking beer and assisting with our communication. That was my first night in Peru. It was comfortable and I slept soundly. It would not always be this way.

Over the next five weeks, I had a series of amazing adventures, all due to the courtesy and wonderful generosity of the warm-hearted Peruvian people. Things were different then in Peru. Lima had no casinos and no U.S. chains or corporate businesses beyond Coca Cola, and Inca Cola was giving them a run for their money. In Cusco, there were very few tour companies and fewer fancy tourist restaurants. The Inca trail was not yet so trendy or internationally famous, and you could hike it practically alone and without a permit.

Machu Picchu

After these five weeks, I still had $28 remaining. Then, teaming up with two other American students, a fellow from Mexico and two Peruvians from Lima, I began to hike the Inca trail from Ollontaytambo to Machu Picchu. After a few days we arrived at an excavation of what might have been the farming village that once supplied mighty Machu Picchu. It is named *Winay Wayna*, which means "forever young." At this time there was no visitor's center because it had only recently been discovered and the rainy season made further clearing impossible. There we set up camp. Our campsite was a bit off and hidden from the Inca trail; Nariano, one of my companions from Peru, knew the location.

The first night, after setting up camp, we all hiked into Machu Picchu. Once there, Nariano gave us a personalized tour. He had been at the location several times and knew all the highlights. Machu Picchu was not yet a mecca for the jet setters. There were no guards at night, so we walked right in and had the place to ourselves. We went back to the camp at 1:00 A.M. and slept for about five hours before we all got up and shared breakfast. Then my traveling friends packed up their gear and went off up the trail, to destinations and adventures unknown. They asked me to join them, but I felt drawn to stay in this special place and wanted to spend all of my remaining time in Peru there.

Once they left, I realized that I only had two loaves of bread and one canteen of water left. I resolved to make these last for as long as I could. I reflected on my adventures in Peru up to this point. There was a strange combination of feeling as if I had returned to a home I had never known along with a deep awe at the unique wonders, beauty, and stark contrasts of this country and it's people. Until this point I had never had such amazing experiences in my life. I was fairly exhausted from having eaten reduced rations for most of my journey, from traveling mostly alone in a very foreign country for five weeks, and from the arduous hike up the Inca trail. All of this would have an effect on my experiences over the next few days; to what degree, I still am not sure.

I went back to Machu Picchu later that morning, tagging along with a professional tour. It filled in some of the information that Nariano had missed. The tour soon broke up and the people departed. That was to be my last contact with other humans for days.

After noon, I went back to my camp. It was drizzling, and I moved my backpack and sleeping roll into a nearby cave. It was circular, large enough to stand in, and about 12 feet wide. The view from the opening was of the clouds and the snow-covered mountain tops of the Andean peaks. It was almost as though I was camping in a different world.

The Gods

That first afternoon after my friends left, I laid down in my sleeping bag and slept until late into the night. I had dreams that I was communicating with the Incan Gods and Goddesses. These fantastic beings told me that I had a karmic bond with Peru. They instructed me to forget my old identity, forget my old life, stay in Peru, dedicate myself to them, and begin a new life. They were embracing yet stern and angry, with powers and abilities that inspired awe and fear. They told me that I had lived in Peru at a time in the distant past. At that time, I had agreed to dedicate a future life to the Incan Gods and Goddesses. In my current incarnation as Michael Peter Langevin, student and spiritual seeker from New England, it was time to pay this debt.

I awoke after midnight, asking unanswerable questions: For what purpose had I been born? Were these truly Gods who had chosen to speak with me? Why me? Did I dare to disobey Gods? And why did I have to return home, anyway?

I felt driven to hike again to Machu Picchu. Upon arriving at the ruins my movements became jerky; my body seemed to want to go different ways than my mind. I walked to the center of the main grassy area, knelt down on the end of the rock that is embedded in the ground there, bowed my head to the peak called Machu Picchu, and mumbled something. It was unclear to me what I was saying. I then turned and knelt facing Wayna Picchu and put my head to the ground and mumbled again. I got up and turned, first toward the east and then toward the west, then repeated the process. After about a half an hour of this, I began to run around the site looking into corners and touching everything. I did this all night, laughing and mumbling. At sunrise I sat at the hitching post of the sun and watched a glorious sunrise over the mountains. Then before people came I hiked back to my cave at Winay Wayna. I had a few bites of bread and a sip of water, got back into my sleeping bag and fell asleep instantly.

It appeared as though my time at Machu Picchu the evening before had tuned up my dream receptors, turning them into an enhanced astral reality. On the other side of the door of consciousness waited the Incan Goddesses and Gods. The detail of my perception was intimidating; these were truly radiant God beings! There was a glowing presence, which I took to be Wiracocha, their Creator God. There was also a fiery figure that I assumed was Inti, the Sun God. Pacha Mama, the Earth Goddess, was easy. She appeared as a beautiful Inca Maiden, but she felt as-all encompassing as the Earth itself. Mama Occala, the Goddess of Water, was a woman with skin like fish scales and seaweed for hair. Yet somehow she was still unimaginably sensual. Liviac, the Lightning God, was a living bolt of lightning, while Pacsa Mama, the Moon Goddess, appeared in beautiful rays of silver, seeming a bit more pregnant each night. Chuqui Yllayllapa, the Thunder God, appeared as a fierce royal Inca warrior who could explode in a huge thunderclap. Ch'aska is the Inca messenger, and Venues is the planet with smoking hair. She is the Goddess represented by the evening star, the morning star and the dawn. I have only mentioned the major players of this extensive pantheon. Most of the Goddesses and Gods can alter their form from pure light (the natural aspect of their godhood) to an accessible, human-like form.

These Gods and Goddesses once again informed me of my responsibility to Peru. They were angrier than in the dream from the night before, insisting that I was attempting to cheat them. They made it clear that they were not to be denied. "You promised to help the children of the empire," they said. "You agreed to assist in bringing about Earth's golden age, with Peru as its center. Do not go back on your word or the consequences will be devastating."

I awoke again at midnight, feeling more confused and even less like myself. I hiked back to Machu Picchu and repeated the same strange rituals and prayers. My body was responding to a deep understanding that went far beyond conventional notions of knowledge. It seemed I was reciting prayers in the Quechuen language, but I still didn't know Quechuen nor the meanings of what I said. I knelt down, facing Wayna Piccu, and prayed. I then got up, turned toward the east, and prayed for coca leaves and passion. Then, turning to the west, I prayed for calm seas in my life, adaptability, and strength. I rose and began to dance, better than I had ever danced before or since, and sang a sad, high-pitched Quechuen song. After about two hours of this dancing and singing, I began to walk from one structure to another, kneeling and praying that I might remember the details of each beautiful structure. By sunrise, I was crying with joy and confusion.

I went back to my cave and experienced my third set of intense Incan dreams. They began much like the first two. In the dream, I awoke in an ancient Incan city, all alone. I stood up and began walking towards the music of panpipes. The building felt as if it might be a temple, with a thatched roof and exquisitely chiseled stone. Everywhere were statues, paintings, vases, and weavings placed in a sparse enough way as to draw attention to each other-worldly work of fine craftsmanship and art.

I eventually found the source of the music. There were twelve couples sitting around an extensive and radiant weaving, near a balcony that overlooked an idyllic scene of rolling terraced hills, accented with streams and rivers. The sun was shining brightly, yet I could see the moon and stars as well. It was fairly cool, and there was a fire burning brightly in the corner of the dining hall. One man stood up to face me. He spoke in Quechuen, but somehow I understood the words.

"I am Manco Copac—the first Inca. Here with me are the major Sapa Incas and their queens. We have worked out our differences and sit together on occasion to help shepherd the future of our children and our empire. You, Partiri, may or may not be welcomed at our meal today; talk with us and we shall see." I did not know the name that he had called me, but it felt comfortable, like an old and familiar robe that I was wearing again after many, many years.

He sat back down, and a beautiful woman rose to address me. "I am Mama Coya, the first Inca's wife, and I must know what you recall of your lives, pledges, and promises as an Inca."

My heart was frozen with a wrenching fear. "My lady," I stammered, "I must confess that I remember nothing of my past lives or promises. I am deeply sorry."

Next stood a tall and intimidating Inca. "I am Pachacuteq," he said. "In one life we were friends. I had high hopes for you and your willingness and abilities to experiment with spirituality and soul transmutation. You taught many things to me and my advisors. Partiri, teach us now. What game do you now play, and how will it aid our children?"

I was physically shaking, and my hunger and thirst were all consuming. "Pachacuteq, I am greatly honored to speak with you. Yet I must confess, you must have me confused with another. My name is Michael Peter Langevin. I grew up in Methuen, Massachusetts in the United States. I want to help the poor and disenfranchised of Latin America as Che Guevera attempted to, but I have never before been to Peru and I am unsure how to help you. Maybe some food and drink would help."

"Fool! Liar! Failure! Why did we bother?" Pachacuteq sat down and another warrior stood up.

"I am the Sapa Inca Wiracocha, Pachicuti's father. In all ways except for fathering him, I failed the Empire. I understand confusion and fear in times of great need. Here, eat this cuy (guinea pig) and drink this chica (corn beer) with us. I know now what I should have done differently in my life. You, too, must remember now what you should do for the good of the future. You and others like you were given great rewards in the past; in exchange, you agreed to undergo an incantation of great pain and torture so that you might visit possible futures, return at a key juncture, and aid in making the Inca dream a reality."

I ate the food that he offered. It tasted awful and indescribably good all at once. Then I took a big gulp of the chica, the traditional Incan corn beer. This was the wrong thing to do! I fell over frozen in waves of ecstasy. I wanted to stand and speak but I was spinning and floating and everything dissolved into a wave of chaos. When I awoke in my cave the sun was low. I felt full and scared and excited as I wrote in my journal: "What dreams I am having here! Wow! Over a month in the most foreign land I have ever seen, and high altitudes and isolation and dreams that put comic books to shame. I, Partiri, the savior of the Peruvian people and the realization of the Inca dreams . . . right! Delusions of grandeur and the dreams to match. Well, back to Machu Picchu before the twilight is totally gone."

I got there as the darkness came on. I walked right to the center of the complex, knelt, and began to pray: "Powers who will listen and take effect, God, Jesus, Mary, John the Baptist, St. Anthony, angels, Buddha, Mohammed . . . Inca Gods and Goddesses, Sapa Incas and your Queens, please help me! I am afraid! I want to do great things and save the world but I'm not even sure why I came to Peru. Maybe I am going crazy or maybe I am more than I had ever previously suspected. I don't want to fail in the great mission that the Gods and Goddesses have put before me. But what am I supposed to do? God, Jesus, I know that you are not the jealous Gods that they teach of in church. You are living Gods who man has often misquoted and misused. Do these Inca Goddesses and Gods really exist? Did I make a deal? Please help me find my path."

As I completed my prayer, an unseen force tackled me to the ground. The wind had left my lungs; my head hurt. I wiped some blood from my quivering lip and slowly got back up. But I was again forced to my knees and my head forced to the ground. I began to yell words that sounded like the Quechuen that the Sapa Incas had spoken. I did this facing each direction. Was I praying or demanding? And what was I asking for? I felt close to a breakthrough, warm and tingly, almost drunk or confused, but somehow joyful. The details of who I had once been seemed to be starting to seep into my memories, lingering on the tip of my mind. I prayed again and danced about the ruins. Although not a dancer, I felt that if I could perform this dance on stage, I would become world famous. Although not a singer, the tune I sang was lovely and melodious. I couldn't comprehend how I was doing these things. At one point I was sweating profusely and my lungs and body ached, but I swore I heard the most beautiful music the world has ever known. I ran, bounded, leaped, halted, moved ritualistically, and then I knew it, what ever it was, had come to an end.

I reached the cave again in an exhausted state of bliss. I didn't even have the chance to get into my sleeping bag. I just fell on top of it and passed out. In this, my fourth set of dreams, I found myself disoriented and in a war zone. The Gods and Goddesses, and the Sapa Incas and their queens, were fighting alongside Inca warriors, battling Spanish conquistadors. I was terrified. Sweating and bleeding from cuts and small wounds, I made my way from the battle front to a deserted hillside. My attempts to wake up, or at least tell myself I was only dreaming, were to no avail. I was in a war!

A beautiful Inca woman came and sat beside me. "Hello Partiri," she said. "Do you remember me?"

"I'm sorry," I replied. "I wish to remember, but I cannot."

A tear came to her eye. "Then you have failed in your quest! I am Machota, and we have been soul mates throughout many lives. We were to meet again as lovers, raise a family, and help return Peru and the Incan people to their destined role of world healers. I am alive in another incarnation in your homeland waiting for you, now." Despite her sadness, she kissed me passionately and we began to make love.

The war continued in the background. After an endless time of bliss, I was grabbed roughly and held by two warriors while a fierce warrior stood in front of me. "Partiri, you deserve no love and will receive no fulfillment. To have sex with this slut while your people suffer and lose their lives in endless battles is inexcusable. Your people need you now!"

Then he stuck me with a sharp weapon. My chest ripped open and I thought I would die. "I am Tupac Amaru," he said, "the rebellious Inca leader. I lived a life of constant suffering and pain. You were to make it so others didn't have to. You are failing. Wake up! Quit your silly pampered life of European indulgence. Stay in Peru, rededicate your life to bringing back the Inca destiny or you and all you love will suffer and know only loss and disappointment for eternity."

Then I was fighting naked with a club against Spanish soldiers on horseback with swords. They would hack at me, and I would fall in searing pain. I would pass out and reawaken only to be stabbed by them again. They would stampede me with their horses, and then pull out my tongue and eyes. After countless painful deaths, I awoke on top of my sleeping bag. I had wet it. I was crying and aching and unsure of my sanity. I ate some bread and drank some water. I attempted to clean my sleeping bag and hung it out to dry. Then I sat against a tree staring at the clouds on the mountaintops, afraid to close my eyes or even to move until it began to get dark.

With nightfall came a wave of relief. A sweet, comforting voice told me there was still a slight chance for me to fulfill my destiny. I stood up, got my flashlight, and hiked into Machu Picchu. When I got there, I did not stop to pray in the center; instead, I crossed the ruins to the trail, and proceeded to hike up the mountain Wayna Picchu by flashlight. It took me almost three hours.

The Initiation

I sat at the top of the peak in what is called the Condors Throne. Exhausted, freezing, and frustrated, I lay there shaking, feeling as if waves of ocean waters were pouring over me. It felt as if I was being filled up with warm honey or liquid gold, or bathing in a healing hot spring. After sitting there for almost three hours, I stood up and mumbled "Lo, though I walk through the valley of the shadow of death I shall fear no evil." Then, with a clear mind, I hiked back down. I wanted to go to the Temple of the Moon but could not make myself. Rather I hiked back to my cave and got there before the sun brightened again.

I was exhausted and aching, too afraid to sleep and too tired to write in my journal. I ate a bit of bread and had a few swallows of water. At this point, both were almost gone. I sat with my back to the cave wall, wrapped in my sleeping bag, and stared out the cave door. I was partially convinced I had gone completely crazy. Certainly it was time to go home, yet I couldn't leave before making peace with the Gods. I fought against sleep, but to no avail.

I found myself surrounded by the Inca deities. Inti, the Sun God, spoke. "Your resistance is sheer stupidity. Agree tonight to abandon your useless, weak excuse of a life in Boston and hike down from here to begin your life anew in Peru. Say yes and you might be able to aid us in our future. Say no and we have no choice but to curse you and all those you claim to love. Watch how it will be!" He stepped aside to reveal my family, friends, teachers, bosses, even the beautiful Inca maiden from the night before. They were all being killed in horrible ways, burned with hot metal, pushed over cliffs, even raped or pulled apart by horses. I cried and begged and screamed. For what seemed like days I watched and endured their torture at the hands of the Gods and Goddesses. Eventually, with excruciating slowness, they each died at the hands of these evil beings.

When finally my parents were killed in front of my dreaming eyes, I broke into tears, sobbing repeatedly, "No, no! Bring them back! I will do anything! Do not torture them, do not kill them. I love them more than life itself." I awoke to tears again, but in my mind I heard voices whispering instructions: "You must agree fully, mean what you promise, and dedicate your life to us, or the visions that you have seen will come to pass."

It was nearly nightfall. I grabbed my flashlight and began to hike back to Machu Picchu. I reached the

Serpent's Tooth, an Incan stone gate and watch wall that overlooks the ruins. Below were shadowy figures and lights, in all likelihood, a nighttime guided tour. But in my state, with a loosening grip on reality, I imagined it was the Gods waiting to continue my torture. "Oh no you don't," I said, in a shaky voice. "I refuse to suffer any more at your cruel hands!" I turned around and headed back to the relative safety of my cave.

By that point, my hunger and thirst were extreme. I finish my first small loaf of bread but left the second untouched. That uneaten loaf was my only remaining food. I poured the last of my water into the frying pan and pot, and searched the cave site for plants that looked edible. I found a small amount of safe-looking jungle plants, started a fire, and boiled them as the sky grew bright. I took it off the fire to cool while attempting to summon the nerve to eat it. Meanwhile, my eyes fell upon the fire; the Gods and Goddesses seemed to be dancing in the flames, laughing and torturing my loved ones. Liviac, the Lightning God and Chuqui Yllayllapa, the Thunder God, looked out at me and said "Partiri, you have failed! We are unforgiving, and now you must suffer forever."

This stoked my fears, even as it stirred my anger. "No!" I yelled out loud. "I have not failed! You will no longer torture me with your horrible visions. Perhaps I do belong in Peru now! I will not stay, but I swear that I will show you. I have a great destiny and you will help, not hinder me in my path!"

The Compromise

The day was hot and sunny; as the sun slowly made its way across the sky, my stomach growled. My throat was parched beyond description. When the cool evening finally arrived, I left the cave and looked for water.

Eventually I found a small puddle, into which I soaked my handkerchief. I sucked the liquid from the rag, but spit it out immediately. It was animal urine, probably from a llama. In my anger and despair, I swore that I heard the Gods' cruel laughter.

I went into the cave, put my last loaf of bread between the cave wall and myself, and fell back into the terrifying world of my Incan nightmares. In this dream, it was night and I was back in the Inca temple. The gathering at the feast was much bigger, for many of the Gods and Goddesses had joined the Sapa Incas and their queens. They were all eating and talking as they ate. I screamed! They all became quiet and looked at me.

"No more! You win! I will make a deal! I have failed; I am weak and not yet a warrior by your standards. If I stayed I would only fail you further. I am going back to Boston, and to school. I will finish my education, find my path, and learn to become a warrior in my own way, in my own life and time. Then I will come back and fulfill the promises that I have carried into this plane of existence. If you spare my family, friends, and loved ones and if you help me to overcome my forgetfulness and weakness, then I pledge to rededicate my life to you."

The Supreme Creator, Wirachoca, came to me as a fierce Inca warrior with Pacha Mama, Mother Earth, on one side and Inti, the Sun God, on the other. "This is not what we agreed to in past lives," he said, with an angry look upon his face.

However, in my feverish hunger and thirst, I stood up and looked him squarely in the eye. "I am sorry. This is the best that I can offer in this life. I am still not sure I am who you think I am. I know I can't do what you want right now. But I am honored to be chosen by you. I will promise to do everything I can to help bring about the rise of the Inca spirit on Earth today. But I must be allowed to find the ways that work best for me. Do you accept my promise?"

Pacha Mama then asked. "If we refuse?"

"Then I will leave anyway. You will do what you will. But I will never return to Peru nor even attempt to help. And I will know you are only evil torturous Gods, nothing more."

Then Ch'aska landed in bird form on my shoulder. "Then we agree. We will ruin you if you attempt to betray us yet again, but we will give you your way and attempt to aid you if you hold firm to these new promises. My sister the humming bird will become your guide." After stating my promises in this fever-like dream, I felt Pacha Mama step close to me, reach into my chest, and pluck out my heart. She bit out a large chunk and swallowed it.

"Your heart is mine," she said. "The deal is of your making."

The next morning, I awoke to find that my last loaf of bread had one large bite taken out of it. I stood there in my cave entrance and yelled to the Andean peaks: "Peru, Inca Gods and Goddesses, whoever or whatever you really are, I am leaving here today. But I will return, and we will do important work together, as I have sworn."

I am convinced that these experiences were much more than vivid nightmares and imaginings. They were a lucid visitation with extra-dimensional Godlike beings of Inca mythology. While in Machu Picchu, some nearly unexplainable bond was forged between myself, Peru, and the Inca Gods and Goddesses. I know and feel it to be true.

Thus ended my first journey to Peru, and began the journey of my life's work. I realize now that many of the rituals that I practiced during that week, both in the cave as well as in the ruins of Machu Picchu, were, in fact, traditional Inca rites of ancient standing. How did I know them then? I can only offer my opinion that the Gods and Goddesses communicated these things to me through my wild, scarifying dreams.

My initiation into the traditions and mysteries of the Incas started then. In my studies and return trips to Peru over these intervening years, I have been blessed in countless ways. I often wake up with partial memories of the Inca Gods and Goddesses either telling me something, teaching me something, warning me, or scolding me for moving too slowly or for not doing what they think I should. These dreams have become my guideposts and have kept me firmly on the Inca Trail, regardless of where I am.

Much of what I have learned about Peru, the Inca people, and their ancient rituals will be found in the pages to come. Together we will explore what it means to be an Inca in modern society, and learn how to bring the majestic, beautiful, and simple wisdom of the Inca culture into the hustle and bustle of our lives. We will look at the history of this great people, which spans at least a thousand years into the past, and will stretch forward thousands of years into the future. Even more, we will talk of the all-powerful Inca Gods and Goddesses, and explore why their presence is felt as greatly today as ever before.

In showing you these things, I hope to fulfill at least some of the promises made by that young man in 1973. And I also hope to help you fulfill some of the promises that you may have been making to yourself, to open your heart and your mind to possibilities and challenges that you might scarcely believe could exist. There is an energetic quality to the people of Peru and the Inca culture that I truly believe can save our world, if we only will allow it. There is no better time than right now to embrace this wonderful and unique opportunity.

Are you ready to begin?

1
Who Were the Incas?

Journal Entry—September 6th, 2001: It is 28 years since I first visited Peru, and 11 years since my wife Deborah (whom I am convinced was Machota, in a past life) and I adopted our children Henry and Sophia from that magical land. Finding them and becoming a family was another important step toward fulfilling my long-standing promises to the Inca Gods and Goddesses.

Now the four of us are on an airplane, returning to Peru once again. It is strange to be flying back with my wife and two mature yet young children. Peru can be a challenging country, full of surprises; I do hope that I am not putting any of us at risk. However, when we became a family, Deborah and I promised we would return before the children became teenagers, to live back in their homeland for a prolonged visit. Now Henry is 13 and Sophia just turned 12, and we are keeping our word.

My children have many confused ideas about what Peru is really like.

They are also wondering what it means to be of Peruvian descent, yet be raised by two parents of European heritage in California. I hope that this extended stay in the land of their birth will answer some of their questions, and allow them to see for themselves the people, places, and culture that make their homeland so special.

We're beginning our descent now into Lima airport. I can't help but marvel at the beauty and diversity of the land beneath me: majestic mountains and beautiful beaches, lush forests and rolling plains, tiny villages and massive cities. All combine to form the Peru of today, not so different from the Peru of 1973, and not even so different from the Peru of a thousand years ago *or more. The land, as much as anything, has shaped the Incan people throughout their long and illustrious history.*

I have resolved to write a book that shares the wonders, mysteries, rites, rituals, and magic of Peru and the Incan people. At the high point of their influence and power, they were a uniquely advanced culture. Many of their beliefs survive to this day. The Incas had (and still have) an incredibly powerful belief system and spiritual practice that can greatly enhance anyone's life. But first, the Incas of the past, the present, and the future must be understood.

This will be the mission of the next four months of my life.

How Old Is the Incan Culture?

Who were the Incas? It's a difficult question to answer, because much of their history is shrouded in mystery and lost in legends. Many scientists, anthropologists, and archaeologists disagree on the details of their emergence; in fact, the period of time that humans have been living in the Americas is a subject of intense debate. Did they arrive over the so-called land-bridge over the Bering Strait 10,000 years ago, or have humans been living in South America for an excess of 40,000 years? Conservative archaeologists who study ruins and ancient trash heaps, as well as anthropologists who study social evolution, seem to agree that there were civilized humans in the Andean region dating back to at least 10,000 B.C.E. The Incan Empire is thought by many to have existed from approximately 1100 C.E. to 1533 C.E., a span of less than 500 years. Others however feel that the 12 legendary pre-Spanish rulers, called Sapa Incas, might have symbolized a lineage of emperors that stretches back far into antiquity. It is true that before the Sapa Inca Pachacuteq's rise to power in 1438 C.E., all previous history seems to be based on myths and legends. It is certainly quite difficult to undeniably substantiate any of these legends. Yet it is undeniable that the Incas were the culmination of all the Andean cultures that predated them. The Tewunaku, Chavin, Nasca, Mocha, Wari, Chimu, Chachapoyas, and many others contributed to accomplishments for which the Incas are today known.

Few Westerners realize that we owe the ancient Incas and their Andean ancestors for countless varieties of corn and potatoes. Among them, the white potato is a staple in most Western homes. They also gave us many useful drugs, among them quinine and coca, which the Incas used mostly in rituals. Their civilization was remarkable and unique in terms of inventive genius, artistic ability, creativity, and an agricultural knowledge that has never been surpassed. Their intricate weavings and beautiful pottery equal anything made in contemporary Egypt, Greece, Rome, or China.

The Territory

The Andes mountain range made up the backbone of the Incan Empire's land mass. The Andes are actually the largest mountain range in the world, covering 7,500 kilometers (approximately 5,000 square miles). The Himalayas have some taller mountains, especially Everest and K2, but some of the mountains of the Andes have heights of between 3,000 and 4,000 meters or approximately 9,000 to 12,000 feet. Huascaran, at 6,768 meters or 22,200 feet is Peru's highest mountain and the world's largest tropical peak. The terrain of the Andes is predominantly made up of the altiplano, an area of high altitude where only small shrubs or grasses can grow. This area features a harsh climate and a soil that resembles peat moss. By developing and adapting crops, agricultural techniques, and domesticating animals that could prosper in these environments, the Incas were able to feed an extensive well-populated Empire. The Incas were fantastic in their ability to adapt cultural advances from various other Andean cultures and modify them to fit the needs of a huge Empire. They adapted their agriculture, statesmanship, political and military organizations as well as their art and architecture to fit their land. Nothing was lost or overlooked if the Incas might utilize it for the good of their people.

As well as the Andes, the Incan Empire had a lengthy coastline stretching from present-day Colombia in the north to the middle of Chile in the south. It had extensive rich coasts from which extended broad desert areas broken up by many fertile river valley oases. The Empire had all of these varied and rich environments, but the nearly unconquerable Amazon jungle was the spice that gave the empire its true flavor. It was the leaven that raised the dough of possibilities for the Incas. The Amazon was among the most difficult areas for the Incas to conquer and one of the hardest portions of the empire to keep loyal. It is speculated that the city of Machu Picchu was built on the edge of the jungle as the place that spiritual offerings were made before the Incan emissaries journeyed into the Amazon. The jungle is all magic, challenge, and mystery. It supplied exotic feathers of macaw and parrots, as well as rare pelts of jaguars, monkeys, and tapirs. Many if not most of the Inca's herbal cures came from the jungle. Once on an eight-hour hike through the Amazon, my guide (who was not a curandero, traditional herbal healer) but just a local resident) showed me trees, plants, and even bugs and worms that could prevent pregnancy, cure malaria, clear up respiratory and breathing discomfort, take the pain out of arthritis, remove wrinkles, keep mosquitoes away, heal infection, cure fevers, hold off hunger and fatigue, heal kidney and liver problems, and aid stomachaches, among other things. It caused me to wonder as I chewed on a white beetle worm taken from inside a hard-shelled nut. The worm tasted like coconut and was supposed to cure lung congestion. I wondered what other cures the Incas had known that have been lost. We can only speculate how many other ways the Amazon jungle influenced the Incan Empire's view of reality.

The Myths

To understand the Incan view of their existence we must be aware of two of their important creation myths. The first concerns the creation of the human race. Wiracocha, the Incan Creator God, caused the sun to emerge from the waters of Lake Titicaca. We refer to this deity as Wiracocha, but the Creator God had many names, titles, and powers attributed to him throughout the Andean regions. He then went to the ancient and deserted lakeside metropolis of Tiwanaku, which in an earlier time had been inhabited by a race of giants called Nawa. Here he gathered primordial clay and modeled animals and people. On the people models, Wiracocha painted different clothes and distinct costumes that would distinguish the many different peoples of the Andes. Each group was instructed in its different languages and customs before being sent to the Earth to reemerge in their new homelands. Wiracocha then reduced himself to human form with a staff and four-pointed hat that have been carried and worn by the Andean priests and astronomers ever since. He began to walk with a blanket carrying gifts for his new people, setting out across the Andes to make sure all was right with his new creations.

The second important creation story involved the founding of the Incan Empire. The founding Incas, Manco Capa and his wife/sister, Mama Occala, emerged from Lake Titicaca at the Island of the Sun. They had been sent to Earth by their parents Inti, the solar Father God, and Mama Quilla, the lunar Mother Goddess, to bring culture to what the Incas claim was a barbarous world. They had been given a golden staff, with instructions to throw it into the ground. Where it sunk beneath the topsoil, there they were to establish their empire. They traveled long and searched hard until they arrived at the Cusco Valley. Here their rod sank beneath the topsoil. Thus, they founded Cusco, which was destined to become the center of the Incan universe.

The Sapa Incas

The first descendants of Manco Capa and Mama Occala were the first eight rulers, known as Sapa Incas. Again, there are some disagreements about their names, dates, and details. The most frequently found names are Manco Capac, Sinchi Roca, Lloque Yapanqui, Mayta Capa Capac, Tupac Yupanqui, Inca Roca, Yahuar Huacac and Wiracocha Inca. For more than four hundred years, they were content to rule mainly the Cusco Valley and some surrounding areas. As each Sapa Inca died, his or her body was mummified. Their mummified bodies were given new homes in Cusco and their relatives took care of them as if they were still living. Every day their clothes were changed and they were given both food and drink. They were carried to visit other mummified Sapa Incas and they were present at most major religious ceremonies.

In truth, only the ruling elite were referred to as Inca, and only they were allowed to wear large gold earrings. However, in this book, I, like many writers before me, have utilized generalizations in referring to all those people who lived in the Empire as Incas. I have also taken some liberties with the word *Inca*, using the plural form *Incas*, and the descriptive term *Incan*. Although neither is completely correct from a grammatical standpoint, they seem much less awkward to my eyes and ears.

In approximately 1438 C.E., everything changed. The Incas' control of the Cusco Valley and the very existence of the Incan people were threatened by the attack of the northern Chanca tribe. The Incas and the Chancas had been at war for some time, although exactly how long is unclear. In that year, events took a turn for the worst. The eighth Sapa Inca, Wiracocha, named after the Incan Creator God, and his chosen heir Inca Urcon fled Cusco and took refuge in the village of Chaca, which is now referred to as Reine. This village is approximately 45 miles south of Cusco. However, Wiracocha's younger son, Yuqanqui, refused to desert Cusco. He remained with the bravest generals and villagers, where they succeeded in defeating the mighty Chanca warriors. This is probably the most legendary Incan triumph. Young Yuqanqui quickly declared himself the ninth Sapa Inca and changed his name to Pachacuteq. He allowed his father to live, although his brother was not so lucky.

Pachacuteq went on to expand and redesign every aspect of the Incan Empire. Thus began one of the most accelerated growth periods of any empire in recorded history. Pachacuteq, his son, and grandson led the Incas in an almost unimaginable military expansion. The Incan Empire became know as Tathuantinsuyo ("Four Quarters of the Universe"). Over the next one hundred years they conquered over six million people and almost a quarter of South America's land area.

Inti the Sun God and Mama Quilla the Moon Goddess had appeared to Pachacuteq in a vision and provided inspiration for the great deeds that he had to accomplish for the betterment of his people. In gratitude, Pachacuteq established the grand Temple of the Sun and Moon in Cusco as the main temple of the Incas. He went on to pass a law that all villages of the Empire must build temples of the sun and the moon as their main places of worship. How one ruler could have accomplished all Pachacuteq is credited with is almost beyond belief and yet it is another area of huge historical debate among authorities of antiquity. However, he is generally credited with rebuilding all of Cusco in the shape of a Puma, conquering the entire Sacred Valley, the heavily populated Lake Titicaca region, and much of northern Peru, and, according to some, building Machu Picchu. He supposedly designed the plan for the Inca trails and highways and the human relay messenger service that allowed him to know everything that happened in his Empire on almost the same day it occurred. Pachacuteq turned over the title Sapa Inca to his son Topa Inca long before his death to ensure that all the rules and laws of statecraft that would guarantee his Empire's survival were clearly stated, understood, and followed throughout the lands.

Topa Inca is referred to as the Alexander the Great of the Incas. From the time he assumed control of the military until the end of his reign, he expanded the empire by 4,000 kilometers, from central Equador to central Chile. After all of Pachacuteq and Topa Inca expansion, Wayna Capa's reign was one mainly of consolidation. Wayna Capa, the eleventh Sapa Inca and the son of Topa Inca, expanded the lands he ruled to the north nearly to

Colombia and further west into Bolivia and the Amazon jungles. His rule, however, and the life of his chosen heir were cut short by the first epidemic of smallpox, believed to have been brought to the Americas by the first Spanish explorers. It is thought to have advanced south from Panama faster than the Spanish themselves. This plague caused the single and most far-reaching loss of life that ever occurred in the Americas. In the first 20 years it is estimated that up to one half of all the Incas perished from smallpox alone. After the death of Wayna Capa, two of his surviving sons fought a civil war for the Sapa Inca title. They nearly destroyed the Empire until Attahualpa captured the throne and executed the other claimant, his brother Huascaran. Attahualpa emerged victorious as the official twelfth Sapa Inca and was marching to retake Cusco when Pizzarro captured, ransomed, and killed him in 1533. Beyond puppet rulers and unsuccessful rebellions, Attahualpa's death was the official end of the Incan Empire. It is natural to wonder what might have been and what was lost when the Spanish terminated the flower of Incan and Andean cultures. Aside from some of their agricultural products, none of their unique aspects have ever truly entered world culture. History moves forward, leaving us with the task of attempting to resurrect what otherwise might become completely lost. This resurrection is what we must focus on.

The Religious Beliefs

It is very challenging to write about the religious beliefs of a people like the Incas. First, there is the difficulty of comprehending their minds, whose thoughts and traditions were entirely different from those of all other nations of the old world. None of the scholars in the field can even agree on dates, reasons, or details of the Incan and pre-Incan worlds, or what they might mean to us today. If I let my mind run to conspiracies, I could be convinced that much of the Earth's past, especially much about the Incas, is being intentionally hidden, to withhold the truth about how long civilizations have existed on Earth or to cover up the huge amounts of powerful information that would allow individuals to discover their fullest potential. However, there have been many good guesses made and much more information emerges every day about the true spirituality of the ancients. Here then is my brief overview of the Incan religious practices and spiritual beliefs.

In the century before the Spanish came, the ritual observances of sun worship at Cusco increased in magnificence with every expansion of the Empire and with each passing year. The splendid Temple of the Sun, named Coraconcha, was rebuilt, as was all of Cusco, by the superhuman feats of Pachacuteq. In terms of beauty and symmetry, it is unsurpassed. The accuracy with which the stones fitted into each other was exquisite. The cornices, the images, and the utensils were all of pure gold. When the Sapa Inca was present, the ceremonies put to shame those of all other earthly kingdoms.

The Religious Offices

The elaborate rituals and ceremonies held at Coraconcha were reflected throughout the Empire and necessitated the employment of an extensive hierarchy, divided into many grades. The High Priest was an official of the highest rank, often the brother of the Sapa Inca. He was called *Uillac Uma*, or "the head which counsels." As supreme judge and arbitrator of all religious questions, he spent his life in religious contemplation and abstinence. He was a strict vegetarian who drank only water and dressed in an ordinary fashion, with a robe flowing to the ankles with a mantel of gray vicuna wool. With the financial support of the state, his responsibilities included the care of those citizens afflicted by blindness or other disabling infirmities. Besides being of illustrious lineage, the high priest was an *Amaute* or "a man of learning." He appointed the visitors and inspectors whose duties were to report on all the temples in the empire. And he appointed the *Ichuri*, which is believed to have been a kind of confessor and assignor of what we might call penance. Under the Uillac Uma there were ten or twelve chief priests in each province called *Uilca*, who had authority over all the numerous *Huacap* or priests and *Huacap Rimachi* or "oracle readers."

Another dominant class in the complicated hierarchy was that of diviners and soothsayers, called *Huatuc*. They dressed in gray, subsisted on roots and herbs, spent most of their waking hours in one temple, and maintained celibacy while holding office. Some Huatuc practiced divination by looking at the flight of birds, while others analyzed the legs of hairy spiders, heaps of maize, or the entrails of sacrificed animals.

The universal belief of all Incas was that all things in nature had a spiritual essence. Prayers and sacrifices were offered to these elements or holy entities, in the hope that good would likely come from such attentions. There was another belief that everything that existed had a spiritual counterpart in another dimension. In other words, whatever was done on the material plane was also carried out on the spiritual plane. This belief explains why the deceased Sapa Incas were clothed and fed and treated as if alive, for then they would be so treated on the spiritual realm.

A Citizen's Life

Spirituality played no less a role for the average Incan citizen. When a baby was born in the Empire, it was almost always immediately given a bath in freezing cold water, and then wrapped in a blanket to keep it warm. It was believed that if it didn't survive this dunking, then it would not have been strong enough to be a good citizen. These babies were all referred to as *wawas* until their naming ceremony, which was not performed until at least their second year, due to the high rate of infant mortality. At the age of 8 to 16 an Incan boy would begin to assist in hunting for his family and working in the fields. At the ages of 10 to 13, the prettiest girls were selected to become *Aclla*, or "virgins of the sun." Those not chosen were able to become wives, weavers, coca-pickers, and assist in the fields. From the ages 16 to 50 all Incas were expected to do hard work in building houses, working the fields, or weaving, as well as maintaining the roads, bridges, and temples in and around their village. Between the age of 50 and 60 they were expected to perform only the labor they felt up to, without repercussions. After the age of 60 they weren't expected to work any more. They were looked upon as wise village elders. They were provided for by their *Ayllu* ("family or clan"), their village, and the state.

The role of women in the Incan Empire was varied. The girls selected as Aclla, known individually as *Intip Chinan* ("the chosen of the Sun"), were looked upon as the blessed of the blessed, for their lives could be dedicated to being close to the Gods. Once picked, these girls served as servants to the elder girls for their first three years. After their apprenticeship, they were taught to perform intricate ceremonial ritual worship to Inti, as well as sew, weave, make fine breads and cakes, sweep and clean the temple and keep the sacred fires (called *Ninu Uilca*) burning. Many priestesses and daughters of nobility were sent to study with the novices, although they were not going to be Aclla. This was done because it was believed to be the most well-rounded training available for young girls. When the Aclla were trained, they were brought before the Sapa Inca and the Uilac Uma or their representatives. Those who wanted to were allowed to stay on as virgins, priestesses, and teachers. Many were given important husbands, and some became concubines to the Sapa Inca and other royalty.

In northern Peru and Ecuador, the Incas did nothing to alter the long-standing practice of matriarchal rule. Both before and after the Incas, the women in these regions were the rulers. They passed on their lineage, they married and bedded whoever they chose, and they made and enforced the laws. This did not change until the Spanish took over. Women also held a great many spiritual roles and offices throughout the Incan Empire. This is borne out by the fact that after the Spanish established control, they began persecuting all those who still practiced, taught, or held native spiritual beliefs. They brought to trial an equal number of women as men for being village native spiritual leaders, teachers, and healers.

The typical Inca endured a harsh life. The Empire enforced strict punishments for all violations of the law. Any crimes against the state were also crimes against the Sapa Inca and thus were considered crimes against the Gods. The punishment was almost always very severe. The Incas didn't believe in jails, so a minor punishment was a public scolding or perhaps an increase in labor. For second offenses, the penalty was often death by hanging, stoning, or being thrown from a cliff. The death penalty was customary for murder, theft, breaking into state storage chambers, damaging bridges, or for entering into the convent of Virgins of the Sun. Laziness was also considered a major crime, because lazy people deprived the whole of society. It was also punishable by death. Locks, theft, and vagrancy were practically unknown before the Spanish came to Peru.

Beyond the death penalty for crimes, human sacrifice was also practiced to placate the deities. That being said, the subject of human sacrifice and its depiction as widespread, even rampant, in Incan society has come under intense scrutiny. A case can be made that it was easier for the Spanish to justify the rape, pillage, enslavement, and destruction of a people if those people were heathens who worshipped the devil and constantly practiced human sacrifice. This sort of European propaganda was used effectively in Africa and also worked in most other places that the Europeans wished to conquer, with the possible exception of Asia.

The subject of human sacrifice is one of the least agreed upon aspects of the religious beliefs and practices of the Incas. The early Catholics claimed there were frequent sacrifices, while some more recent authorities claim that there were no Inca-approved sacrifices. My extensive research indicates that there were, in fact, some sacrifices, however, they were much rarer than previously thought. They were employed only during those few celebrations that required them or as a last resort to appease the Gods. When all else failed and the Incas feared the Gods' wrath, be it in the form of volcanic eruption, floods, droughts, or other potential disasters, then and only then did they resort to human sacrifice.

While living in Cusco I had a conversation with a delightful and intelligent Canadian couple. They were in Cusco to study Spanish and hike the Inca Trail. I quite liked them and their view of the world until we began discussing the Incas. Their image of the Incas was of bloodthirsty killers, who sacrificed humans on a grand scale as part of their daily worship, and of whore mongers who exploited all women to the level of abject slavery. I was quite taken aback by their views, because they were well-educated people. I had to wonder at how many other people shared this view? All signs point to the fact that human sacrifice was much more widespread with the Aztecs of Mexico and in the Colosseum of Rome than in the Incan Empire. Casual observers tend to get the Aztecs and Incan pre-Spanish Empires confused. They were extremely different in multiple ways. However, what is clear is the fact that the Spanish were responsible for killing off more than half of all native peoples in their conquered territories and enslaving the majority of the rest. Under those circumstances, only the highly effective European propaganda could cause the Incas to be the ones that are portrayed as merciless killers, while the Spanish come down to us across the gulf of history as generally civilized and respectable.

The Incan Empire had its darker aspects; however, there is much more to the story. This harsh military state also assumed responsibility for the well-being of all of its citizens. Everyone had to labor a percentage of their time for the state, the temples, and their village. However, when you became too old to work, you were fed and clothed by the state and the temple. They also fed and clothed the sick, the blind, the diseased, and those who, due to accident, could not work. If there was a natural disaster in any part of the Empire the Sapa Inca sent his army with food, clothing, and medical aid, in order to rebuild the damaged villages and damaged lives. There was certainly no reciprocal agreement similar to this in any European nation at that time.

The People's Spirituality

The Incas understood the importance of reciprocity. They also understood their relationship with nature, as well as the power of ritual. They knew that everything has a spirit. They knew how to speak to and work with these spirits. They understood the importance of creativity. They had a special relationship with the sun, the moon, the stars, and lightning. These forces, almost beyond the comprehension of average citizens, required worship and study by scholars and priests. All this combined knowledge and beliefs greatly affected and enhanced the daily lives of all citizens of the Empire.

Pachacuteq's law that every village and city in the Empire should have the largest temples devoted to Inti and Pacsa Occala, above all other Gods or Goddesses, is the ultimate example of how life was viewed by the Incas. The Incas had great symbolic traditions of opposites, of Father and Mother, of Earth and Sky, of Night and Day. The balances and contradictions of the Incan society were all exemplified by these opposites. Balancing the oppositional forces in their lives was at the base of almost all Incan daily actions. The most popular and far-reaching spiritual belief of the Incas was the worship of the founder of each Ayllu, what we would call the neighborhood groups or clans. Each subgroup in a village (there were most often 12) closely shared their own rituals and social events. They usually shared the highest reverence to the God or Goddess who was believed to have founded their Ayllu. Next in their canon of deities were the Apus— Mountain Gods or Spirits that protected and blessed their village area and the ancestors who had passed over but yet remained to advise and assist the Ayllu. There were also a wide variety of nature spirits to which each village prayed. Most importantly, each Ayllu also had a special Huaca, or ancestral God, which its members worshipped in common. This was a God represented by a statue, rock, or sacred place somewhere in or near the village. Smaller, Huacas were in almost every home. The worship of deceased ancestors was called *Paccarisca*. Sara Mama the Corn Goddess was often represented in some ceramic form; Sara Mama might be covered in corn or a vase with corn ears painted all over it. Here prayer and sacrifices were made for fertile fields. Llama Mama and Pacha Mama were often represented as a hollow llama statue or other shaped hollow stone. The cavity in their backs was filled with chica or coca. These were then ceremonially buried in the fields where the llama or alpaca grazed. The figurine was then placed on top of one stone and then covered by another. Every year, a new stone llama was buried under the old one; this placed it ever closer to Pacha Mama. This practice is still prevalent in most highland communities today. Each family, as well, had additional personalized household Gods. Each citizen of the Incan Empire had a special personal deity in whom they trusted and to whom they usually prayed first before all the other Gods, Spirits, and Goddesses.

When the Spanish came with their need to convert these pagans, they had quite a set of challenges. The Incan temples of the Sun and Moon and other lesser temples were easily torn down and cathedrals built over their original sites. But how do you compete with a Mountain Apu? You can't stop the thunder or lightning, rainbows, or the dawn. The memory of ancestors stays strong. If healers actually heal people, if prophets accurately foretell the future, or if rituals seem to have a powerful affect on the bounty of a village's crops, how do you discredit them? Thus, in spite of the Catholic Church's best efforts, laws, Inquisitions, witch trails, grinding of stone Huacas to powder, and burning of ancestral mummies, still the Ayllu beliefs have endured and many beliefs and practices are virtually unaltered to this day.

Others rituals have been subtly and not so subtly integrated into the Church's modern day ceremonies.

To this day many of the Quechuen people who live in the remote rural areas live as subsistent farmers almost exactly as their pre-Incan ancestors did. They herd llamas and alpacas. They raise guinea pigs much as other people raise chickens. They grow a wide variety of potatoes, herbs, and, when possible, corn in their rocky fields. Their homes are built of rock or adobe bricks and only the well-to-do use Spanish roofing tiles; the rest still have thatch roofs. They all wear homespun and woven cloths, and to keep warm they wear self-woven llama wool ponchos and sleep under alpaca blankets. They burn llama dung or mountain peat moss in their fireplaces. Their spiritual practices as well have remained the same, having been passed down from generation to generation.

The Incas had a deep understanding of astronomy, astrology, and prophecy. The Empire, its expansion, and operation was greatly affected by these fields as were the lives of all the individuals in the Empire. Some say it had been predicted that the Spanish would come and conquer long before this actually came to pass. There are those who claim today that these pre-Spanish predictions warned of almost 500 years of sorrow and pain following the invasion. This may be viewed as the ultimate testing of the Incan people, like raw ore turning to gold in a fiery pit. After 500 years, the prediction says, the spirit and the essence of the Puma and the Condor would reawaken. The time for the awakening of the Quechuen people, then, is almost upon us. If these preditions are to be believed, these descendants of the Incas will be the ones to lead the world to a new Golden Age, taking the best of the Inca, Spanish, and world cultures and, through a unique brand of alchemy, creating a society that will be a beacon to the rest of the planet.

2

Becoming a Family

Journal Entry—September 12, 2001: *We have been in Lima for almost a week now, staying at a wonderful bed and breakfast hotel called Casa Serana. The owner/operator is a woman named Serana, of course, who operates the place along with her husband Victor, their two sons, and daughter. Their family is quite warm and friendly, and Henry and Sophia have gotten very close to them. Staying here has helped set a wonderful tone that I hope lasts throughout our extended stay in Peru.*

My children in particular are enjoying Lima, where so many of the people have the same physical features as themselves. It must be difficult for them to live in California, where there are so few people from Peru. Already we have revisited many of the places that were involved in our becoming a family. We went to the Hotel Senorial, where they met Anna, who was working there 11 years ago and greatly assisted us in our first weeks together. Then we visited our second temporary home from 11 years ago, El Patio. There we introduced the children to Olga, the owner, and Damai, her lifelong Quechuen assistant. All three of these people from our past were thrilled and proud to see how Henry and Sophia have grown. The fact that the children speak Spanish and English and are honor students as well as athletes impressed them also.

We also toured the Palace of Justice, where we first met Sophia and where we spent countless hours waiting to meet with judges. This is where the final papers were signed for us to become a family. We located the area where Sophia had been found crying under a tree, in one of Lima's better neighborhoods. This was moving for all of us. Then we went to the orphanage where Henry had lived for six months as a toddler.

Although none of the people who were there at the time remained, those who were working there now were proud to see that a child who began at their orphanage had grown up so well.

Henry and Sophia are beginning to get real places to connect to the stories that they have heard all their lives. This is another magical element of Peru, the capacity for inclusiveness, for warmth, for giving and taking among the like-hearted souls of humanity. My wonderful, smart, and caring children fill me with an endless amount of pride and love. What a joy for me to be able to have my love for my children and my love for this land joined together.

Commitment

From my first trip there, Peru continued to impact my life. Many things changed in the 15 years that followed, but I never stopped thinking about the people of Peru, or the imposing Incan Gods that had extracted their fierce promises from my tortured soul in 1973.

In the interim, I had traveled extensively, searching the world and my heart for a purpose in life. Finally I settled in the San Francisco Bay area and founded the magazine *Magical Blend*, which became the oracle wherein I might ask my deepest questions and interact with seekers like myself.

During this time, I also fell in love. By the winter of 1988, after years of courtship, dating, and living together, I asked Deborah Genito to marry me. Her acceptance had an attachment. "I will marry you," she said, "if we can have children and raise a family."

Commitment to a lover is one thing. Commitment to raising kids is quite something else. This was more than

I had bargained for! Looking for signs about which path to take, I journeyed to Death Valley, fasted, performed fantastic rituals, wrote feverish entries in my journal, and honestly examined my hopes, dreams, fears, and doubts. I analyzed my life and my long-term goals. Where did kids fit in? I went back to Oakland, where Deborah and I talked at great length. We agreed that neither of us needed biological kids. We both felt that there were just too many kids in the world as it was, kids who needed loving homes like those we had enjoyed, and kids who needed a good education.

At that time in the United States, adoptions were very difficult and drawn out, and interracial adoptions were still frowned upon. So we agreed that we would adopt from a Third World country. We were married in July 1989. After a long and glorious honeymoon, we quickly began classes on foreign adoption, which answered many of our questions and concerns. We then proceeded to a home study, at which time we were approved to adopt either one or two children. We were unsure if we could go from no children to two children all at once, but the adoption of two children at one time did seem to involve less expense and less bureaucracy. We then began looking into countries that allowed foreign adoption to parents in their thirties who had only been married for one year. There were waiting lists in Guatemala and Costa Rica. Surprisingly, most African countries didn't allow any adoption, and in the few that did, the process seemed extremely difficult. Korea, once a source of many adoptions, had closed its doors, and China was not allowing them yet. But in the background, waiting in the shadows for me to fulfill my promises, stood Peru. Due to a brutal civil war and unimaginable inflation of 1000 percent, many Peruvian children were in dire need of adoption. I laughed as I heard the Gods calling to me once again.

Peru

It was April 1990 when the dust settled and we first called a social worker in Peru. She told us there was a little boy in an orphanage that was just cleared for adoption. He had been abandoned and no relatives could be found. At that point, he had lived in the orphanage for almost six months and was about a year-and-a-half old. We would have to get there in a week to make it all work. I informed the staff at *Magical Blend* of my intention to take a three-week leave of absence. Deborah did the same at her work. We went through the arduous process of getting all of our required documents approved, quickly packed everything we thought we might need, and, with great excitement, caught a plane to Lima. I do not think either of us slept between the time we first spoke to the social worker and our arrival in Peru. The social worker and her husband met us at the airport. They were taken aback by the number of huge moving boxes we had brought with us. They were full of diapers, baby formula, toys, medicine, and clothes, basically everything one would need to begin raising a toddler.

Lima then was going through desperate times. At every traffic light our social worker's husband would run to the trunk to make sure no one attempted to steal the diapers. They helped book us into our hotel, then took us out for dinner. This was an unofficial interview but we were too excited to realize it. We returned to our hotel late that evening, exhausted from the flight and the excitement. Early the next morning, we were awakened by a call from the social worker. We had passed the interview! She informed us that she had already visited the Palace of Justice, and that we might be able to receive custody of our son that very day. Everything was happening so fast. The social worker arrived and we had breakfast together. As we ate she filled us in on the details. If all went well, we would meet with a judge and a government social worker, both of whom had the power to approve everything and grant us custody of our son. Our son!

The Joining

The Peruvian courts move slowly. We spent hours waiting in the hall of the Palace of Justice for our interviews. While we waited, a worker shepherded a group of small children into the offices. Another worker carried a screaming baby girl. We laughed. She was without question the loudest baby either of us had ever heard. After a while the children left and the baby girl was carried out, still crying as if her life depended on it. We had our first interview, which seemed to go well. Then more waiting. In the meantime, we couldn't help but notice that the screaming baby girl had been brought back to the offices. Much later, when we were finally called back in to sign some papers, we saw one of the workers feeding the loud baby girl bits of a chocolate candy bar and Coca Cola from a spoon. Our social worker had a long discussion with the worker. Then she turned to us. She said, "This baby has been in the police orphanage for over a month. No relatives have been found. She was due to be transferred to the state orphanage, but there is no room. This worker has offered to take her home for tonight, but she is poor and has no extra money to feed her. If you would be willing to adopt her too, I am fairly sure that the judge would be pleased and make the two adoptions go quickly." We examined the baby. Her eyes lacked luster. When we passed our hand before them they did not follow. Deborah said, "What do you think, Michael? She might be blind or worse." I thought about it and said, "If it hadn't been meant to be, then she wouldn't have been offered to us."

The Process

Deborah agreed and the workers began more papers for us to take guardianship of Zila as well. Later, we legally changed her name to Sophia Zila. I was holding her and walking the halls of the Palace of Justice. She was still screaming and I was singing softly to her songs my mother had sung to me as a child. A bureaucrat came out of his office and said, "Keep your child quiet or go outside!" Our child! That hit my heart! She was our daughter! The judge was pleased that we were excited to take custody of Zila, too. She signed the custody papers and we left with the social worker and our crying daughter to pick up our son.

At the orphanage we gave them clothes for Henry to dress in, because there was a shortage of clothes and everything else for the children. When he came out, the clothes were too small. He was a big one-and-a-half-year-old boy, bigger than we had expected. I looked at him and thought, "This is my son!" I gave Sophia to Deborah and knelt down to pick up Henry. He too began to scream, in harmony, with his new sister. It was as if they were competing with one another to see who could cry the loudest and longest. In many ways this competition has never stopped. The orphanage workers attempted to tell us about Henry. He was a sweet, charming, and very physical child, they said, but that was about all the information we got. The social worker bundled us and the two screaming kids into a taxi, but halfway back to the hotel she got out, saying that she was late for another appointment. She told us that our lawyer would meet us at the hotel to sign some papers and help us settle in. This lawyer turned out to be a well-to-do, well-dressed, very proper women who had adopted children herself. She knew the ropes, thanks to the Gods, because we sure didn't. We signed the papers and then we got down to getting the kids washed, fed, and changed; she got her fancy outfit soaking wet and covered in baby formula, not to mention what they did to her hair. It seemed that both the children hated water. Sophia wouldn't stop crying until she had drunk quite a bit of baby formula. Henry had to eat lots of enriched baby porridge to begin to quiet down. By then it was late, but they did finally settle down clutching the toys we had given them. Our exhausted lawyer said goodbye, and we thanked her profusely for her help.

Later that night, when both the children were fully asleep, I went down to the hotel bar, got a couple of big Peruvian beers for Deborah and myself, and brought them back to the room. We were exhausted. We could not believe we had gotten custody of our new son and daughter on our first real day in Peru. We kept talking about them and how excited and lucky we felt. After Deborah fell asleep, I went down to the bar and got another beer. I walked into the central hotel grassy courtyard, drinking, and reflecting. I swore I heard voices, but the courtyard was deserted. The voices sounded like my old friends, the Incan Gods and Goddesses. They said, "At last you have done something! These two are special. You must protect and teach them, and they will teach you in return. They are descendants of the Incas. They have the blood. At last, you can begin to live in two worlds. Be the best father you can for them. They are your family and main responsibility now. The future is in your hands."

I mumbled, "I promise to do my best." Then I went back to the room, admired my new daughter and son as they slept, kissed their foreheads, and went to sleep.

The Return

Making the adoption official took much longer than the three weeks that our social worker had at first led us to believe it would take. The courts dragged on and on and on. A bit past the middle of June, I was fantasizing of going down to the docks and finding a ship captain to smuggle us all out. Deborah and I knew these were our children. We were 100 percent sure we had all agreed to this family before any of us were even born, but the Peruvian courts wouldn't make it all legal. As I got to this point of desperation the bureaucratic roadblocks seemed to begin lifting. By the middle of July the government of Peru provided us with official adoption papers and birth certificates and made the adoptions completely legal. We bid Peru a bittersweet goodbye and flew back to Oakland to begin our new lives as a family. Upon our return, Deborah and I promised that we would return to Peru one day, so our children could get to know the land of their birth.

After over 11 years of being a family, I have to state that facing my fears of commitment, marrying Deborah, and adopting Henry and Sophia are the best things I have done in my life. While Alberto Fujimori was President, he ended the Civil War and inflation as well as Peruvian foreign adoptions. After ten years in office, he absconded to Japan with the majority of the Peruvian treasury. To replace Fujimori, Peru just elected their first freely elected president of fully Quechuen descent,

Alejandro Toledo. What he will or won't do as president remains to be seen.

Regardless of the political background, my family has been a bridge to Peru that I could not have created on my own. This pleases me, just as I imagine it must please the great Incan Gods and Goddesses. I think Deborah is beginning to believe that she, too, has led past lives in Peru. Making Peru my symbolic second homeland has greatly enriched my life and the life of my entire family.

3

Living the Incan Life

Journal Entry—October 3, 2001: We have flown from
Lima, the capital of modern Peru, to Cusco, the legendary center of Incan life and culture. It has been a busy time for us. We
were here only one night before departing by train for Machu
Picchu. We spent three days in the Machu Picchu area, touring
the ruins and soaking in the atmosphere of this uniquely magical place. It was wonderful that my family enjoyed Machu
Picchu as much as I had hoped. We hiked to Wayna Pichu and
to the Temple of the Moon—a particularly demanding hike,
especially when you are unaccustomed to the altitude.

We passed through Cusco again on our way to the Amazon
jungle, where we stayed for almost a week at a lodge about an
hour's boat ride up the river from Puerto Maldonado. The bugs
weren't too bad, and everything else was just magnificent. How
does one sum up a region as vast and overwhelming as the
Amazon? I will tell you that if you haven't looked up into the
Amazon jungle canopy and seen the blue butterflies by day and
the fireflies by night, then you haven't fully lived.

After our excursion into the jungle, we returned to Cusco.
This city was the capital of the old Empire; even today it is
vastly different from the western city that Lima has become.
Cusco's population is predominantly of Quechuen descent, and
many people look like my children. They like that. The influence
of the modern Western world can be found in many places in
Peru, but it is not so dominant outside of Lima.

Cusco is not only a magical city, it is still in many ways an
Incan city. The Conquistadors, the Catholic Church, and modern Western culture have all worked to alter the traditional,
rural, Andean lifestyle, but the customs that have come to this
region in the last five centuries have been changed more than

they have affected change in the hearts of the people. For exam-
ple, the figure of Jesus Christ, in many Peruvian minds, is Inti,
the Sun God. The Mother Mary has evolved into an Apu and
Pacha Mama. Like the Amazon, in the fullness of time the Incas
adapt and reclaim everything. The Incan culture was strong
not merely because of military force, but also because of the
inner strength and faith of the people. If the ways of your
grandparents bring meaning and fulfillment, then why would
you ignore them and embrace less meaningful and unfulfilling
ways of life?

Enriching one's life is a tremendous goal. My family and
Peru have done this for me. I feel strongly that the Incas had a
way of life that, if adapted in full or in part by any of us, would
enrich our existence greatly. What I have attempted to do is
translate and update a few basic techniques that the Incas
employed to achieve balance, dignity, and joy in their lives. I
have increased and refined these techniques over the years. I
present them in such a way that anyone can begin easily, with-
out getting overwhelmed or lost. The goal of this chapter is to
get you started. As the book progresses, the information and
techniques become much more involved, but those in this chap-
ter should get your feet wet and get you comfortably acclimated
to the water. Living the Incan life in the modern world is a chal-
lenge. These techniques are some of the simplest ones to use.

Focusing Your Intent
and Realigning Your Vision

When a village was conquered or absorbed by the Incan
Empire, most often the inhabitants of the village were
moved with a minimum of their possessions to a very
different region. This was done to make the new citizens

more dependent upon the Empire for all resources and protection. It made them much less secure and gave them fewer resources with which to launch a rebellion. Also, at least one child of each village leader, usually the oldest son, was taken to Cusco. This was explained as the best way to train them so that they might become great leaders. It also served as a way to indoctrinate them to the Empire's ways and to hold them as hostages so that a village wouldn't consider rebelling.

Becoming a citizen of the Incan Empire meant redefining yourself. It meant integrating a new expanded definition of who you were. You were no longer only a member of a village; you were part of an extensive Empire. This Empire had new and different beliefs and ways of doing things that you were expected to adapt to.

The new citizens who adapted best were given greater authority and power; those who adapted only acceptably had only an acceptable existence; and those who couldn't adapt well and insisted on rebelling or breaking the Incan laws were pushed off a mountain to their deaths. In our modern world you are given more choices, and the results are more subtle. You may continue to live your life as you have before and, if it works for you or you don't feel the modern Incan path is for you, then you must judge the results. If, however, you are less than content, you may consider trying the traditions of the Inca. To embrace the modern Incan traditions you must make a commitment to re-examine your values and goals, and you must clarify and expand your personal vision for your life.

Vision aligning is one of the most basic yet also one of the most powerful spiritual practices in existence. To realign your vision is to focus your intent. Intent is the conscious act of bringing into focus every aspect of your essence into a set vision, just as a magnifying glass brings together the disparate rays of the sun to light a fire, or a funnel brings a large amount of liquid through a small opening. Most people seldom utilize all their resources to accomplish any task. We are mainly a half-hearted society. We pick at doing things and if it works, fine; if not, we go on to something else. But by purposely rallying all your resources—all of who you are and what you know—for one set of reasons, mountains can be moved. A focused intent is one of the most effective tools in Incan tradition.

To focus your intent and realign your vision you must first make time in your life. It can be done by anyone, even if you work a nine-to-five job or attend school full time. For my focusing and realigning, I personally prefer to drive to a desert and hike away from the roads. I build a fire and fast and meditate for a few days or a week. However, this is an ideal circumstance.

Very few of us, in this day and age, have this luxury of time. The key is to set aside sacred time. If you can't get away for a week, the next best thing is dedicating a weekend to focus your intent and realign your vision. If not a weekend, then dedicating a whole evening can suffice. As a last resort, an hour each night for a few weeks will do. Setting aside time with the clear goals of focusing your intent and realigning your vision is the main requirement. I have worked with students who could only commit to one hour a week. However, their intentions were strong and their commitment was deep. They took that hour at the same time each week, and they successfully focused their intent and effectively realigned their vision.

Once you have set aside uninterrupted time, then you must begin by examining your present day life in detail. Following are some of the questions you may want to begin asking yourself:

1. Why do you live the way you live?

2. What are the things, activities, values, and goals that are most important to you?

3. Which of your values, activities, and goals have you continued holding onto even though they have outlived their effectiveness for you?

The best way to begin answering these questions is by using an ancient Incan tool called the *Quipu* (pronounced *kee-poo*).

The ancient Incas had no written language. Instead they used Quipus, which were knotted strings used as tools. Quipus were used for record-keeping, memory recall, and for recording history. A Quipu was a bundle of strings tied to a stick. The number of strings varied greatly, and the number of strings may have been a code as well. The complete uses of the Quipu by the Incas are not known. The position, color, and length of the cords and knots are known to have represented numbers, words, and ideas. The Spanish priests thought the Quipus that the Incas kept to record their history and visions were the devil's tools. Thus, most pre-Spanish Quipus were burned. There are too few remaining today to recreate the exact meaning of all knots and colors in Quipus.

The Quipu method used by the Incan to realign one's values and focus one's intent was to tie a different colored knot in string or yarn for each thing they were ready to let go of. Later, they would tie a different set of colored knots in a different Quipu for the value, activities, and goals they still felt were valid.

This Quipu technique requires brutal self-examination. All of us do things out of habit. We even hold sacred certain values and goals that no longer have meaning for us. Some students beginning their initiation as modern

Incas are not yet comfortable with the Quipu way of keeping track. It requires development of different ways of thinking and remembering, which is why I advise it so strongly. To change and improve our lives, we must develop new ways of thinking and of viewing reality.

The goal is to examine your life today. What isn't working to your benefit? Of all your beliefs and habits, which are preventing you from furthering your personal growth or development? Why are you holding onto these things if they are holding you back? To truly practice Quipu realignment, you must examine every aspect of your life.

Start by taking a stick or small branch of a comfortable length, perhaps a foot long. Tie twelve different pieces of string or yarn to the branch at one end. Tie a knot for each belief, behavior, or portion of your life whose benefits are questionable. The more knots you tie, the more your life will improve. Every knot must represent some aspect of your behavior that you have outgrown or wish to change. This procedure is best done over a period of time. Each new day should allow you to see your life from a different perspective, and provide new insights. Once you fully understand your outmoded beliefs and behaviors, and have tied a knot for each of them, burn your Quipu. As you do this, repeat the following words:

"Today I begin to truly realign my vision. I must clear out the old me to invite the new me in. I must burn the old nonworking vision to allow my new vision to rise from the ashes of my old life. I now dedicate myself to taking actions, values, and goals that make me a modern Inca—a warrior dedicated to adaptability and change. I call on the spiritual forces and on my future improved self to assist me. I call on the spirits of the wind, the mountains, the rivers, and Pacha Mama. I call on the stars, the moon, and the sun. I call on Mama Occala and

Inti. I now disintegrate and destroy all aspects of my life which no longer work for me. Tonight I become an empty clay pot. I await all the fresh, nutritious, and effective ingredients that will be added to my life. I will craft a newly aligned personal vision that I will live with constantly with focus and intent!"

Now that you have cleared out the ineffective, outgrown aspects of your life, you can begin crafting your new vision. Create a new Quipu that lays out your new vision and your progress in achieving it. First, determine what works in your life now? Do you love your significant other? Do your children bring you great joy? Is your work fulfilling? Are your friends dedicated to personal growth and support your endeavors? Do you still feel that achieving a degree or a promotion is the most meaningful path your life can take? For each thing that is still valid, tie a different colored knot on your Quipu.

When you have finished this ritual, you must begin to ask yourself what new vision you wish to add to your life. Do you want to study every aspect of shamanism? Do you want to travel the world? Do you feel that you want more creativity or joy in your life? For each of these resolutions, tie a knot. As you tie the knot repeat the new resolution 12 times. Now, what do you think you can change this week? Tie more knots. What can you change this month? This year? In five years? In ten years? In 25 years? What do you want to accomplish before you die? After you are dead, what do you want people to say about you? Tie knots for every resolution you make. The scope of your imagination is your only limit!

You can, at any moment, change every aspect of your life. Remember the conquered villages that moved hundreds of miles and the young children who had to live and study in Cusco? You can be that extreme. However, you can also set up a series of baby steps. Small changes built and maintained regularly work best for many people. Small changes might seem like: "Today I will cut back my TV watching by one hour," or "I will cut back one junk food meal a week," or "I will drink one less alcoholic beverage a week." Use these mind and spirit exercises to re-examine your life and the vision you are living. Is it your true vision? Is it a vision that will bring you true fulfillment, make you happy, and allow you to fully express your creative side? If not, then craft a new one, and set out a plan to achieve it.

When you feel you have your new vision, it is time to realign it as a modern Inca. It is best to do this alone by a fire or with a candle. Then, touch each knot of your new vision Quipu. With each knot recite that aspect of your life that works or the action you plan to take to create your new life's vision. Call on all the spiritual support you can think of for help and blessing. Then end with:

"May these things or better grow in my life and may my new realigned vision give me the best possible life as a modern Inca."

I religiously re-examine my values, realign my vision, and refocus my intent at least annually. Some years I revisit my realigned vision every three months. As I gain new insights or adjust my vision, I tie new knots. I also cut out knots that I have achieved. The Quipu is a living dream keeper. Use it to serve you in achieving and realigning with your highest vision.

Finding a Nature Spirit Guide

A very simple yet effective place to begin developing your modern Incan magic is to discover your nature spirit guide. In ancient Peru, most people had an animal, plant, or place that was sacred to them. To see one's nature spirit guide was a great sign. There were powerful ceremonies associated with meditating on your nature spirit guide. Some people are blessed; when they hear that we all have a nature spirit guide, they just instantly know what theirs is. Some are told by teachers, friends, or relatives. Others reach a time in their life when they want a nature spirit guide and have none. These people can find one in a vision quest or by asking for it in a dream or even by walking down a city street.

I had a friend who got his nature spirit guide that way. It was a pigeon. I thought that was odd, but my friend tells the following story: While on a city walk in search of his nature spirit guide, he came to a traffic light across a busy street. He looked up and watched as the light turned green in front of him. Just as he began to cross, a pigeon flew right into his face. He jumped out of the way back onto the curb. Just then a car at top speed ran its red light; if the pigeon hadn't flown at him, clearly he would have been hit and killed. He had gone on a city walk in search of his nature spirit guide, and a pigeon saved him from a car that ran a red light. It was a clear sign. Whenever he was near danger, he would see or get a strong feeling of a pigeon.

You can find your nature spirit guide in a number of ways. You can meditate by yourself in a quiet place and let your spirit give you a nature spirit guide in the form of a thought or suggestion. Or, you can go on a nature spirit guide walk. That is a walk dedicated to being open and aware, to the best of your abilities, for what the world is showing you. Taking a nature spirit guide walk in a wild place is best, but a large park or zoo will do. Even walking in the city is fine, as my pigeon-sensing friend will tell you. The key is to stay open to any sign or symbol that you encounter. It is all right if you fear you might be making something up or choosing for yourself.

If your choice is correct, it will add to your life greatly. If your choice is incorrect, then it won't hurt you; it just won't add much to your life. As time goes by, most modern Incas add to their nature spirit guides and end up having as many as ten to call upon.

One of my nature spirit guides is a hummingbird. They come to cheer me up and to point the way for me. They also bring me good luck or warnings. I have had many dreams with hummingbirds teaching me wonderful lessons. May you too have good luck meeting your nature spirit guide. It's easy and fun. Just relax and let your nature spirit guide come to you.

The Power of Nature Spirits

All of nature has spirits. These spirits are powerful. In the Incan time the llamas, guinea pigs, condors, snakes, and pumas were among the best-known and most frequently called upon animal spirits.

Anyone who has shared their life with an animal companion—be it a cow, horse, pig, rabbit, chicken, dog, cat, hamster, fish, tarantula, or scorpion—knows that those animals acknowledge you and await your return. Often they will even comfort you in times of depression or sadness.

The ancient Incan villagers, as with many small farmers throughout history and even today, kept their guinea pigs and baby llamas right in their homes for their animals' safety. In this way, the bond with their animals became as strong as family. This lead to deep understanding and communication.

If you have spent prolonged time out in nature, you have felt a similar but somewhat different connection with the birds, reptiles, and mammals of the wild. They live with a different kind of connection to Pacha Mama and the cycles of existence. Yet, if you see the same animal every few days, you can develop a deep connection. There is much nonverbal magic that animals can teach us. You must personally figure out how to learn it.

The Incas believed the llamas and condors held the spirit of the Andes Mountains, the backbone of the Empire. To be a shepherd to the llamas and to study the ways of the condor were paths that could lead to great wisdom. Shamans of the Amazon held jaguars and anacondas more sacred. These jungle shamans, especially, have many tales of shape shifting. Shape shifting occurs when, through magic and communion with an animal spirit, a being can actually take on the form of that animal. This technique is not a fairy tale—it is doable and has been performed by powerful magic workers throughout time. Shamans understood how to shift their intention points to be able to take on different forms.

Spirits of deceased animal companions are still called upon to bring insights, blessings, or signs. We are surrounded by beings who wish to support and assist our magical growth. Utilize the animal spirit wisely. Although animals do, without a doubt, possess souls, they experience emotions differently than humans do. They can help us with our emotions but we must fully understand the emotions within ourselves.

Emotional Energies

The fact that no written records were kept by the Incas means everything we know was either recorded in European languages or was handed down for many centuries in the oral tradition. Western thought and interpretation have affected much of the information that has come to us. Yet, it seems that there existed in the Incan and pre-Incan people an understanding and use of emotions that is extremely different from what we know today. Emotions were viewed as energies.

In Quechua, the language of the Incas (which their descendants still use today), there are 32 words for our word *light*. There was the morning sunlight, the light given off by fire, by lightning, by the moon, by fireflies, at twilight, and so on.

Emotions, too, were understood by the shamans and priests and used as powerful energies to accomplish many goals. Emotions were valued as tools that were unique to humans, with which they could accomplish most things. Emotions can be separated into those that feel pleasant and those that feel unpleasant. Joy, fulfillment, love, and excitement are some of the pleasant ones, whereas fear, guilt, hate, anger, jealousy, and frustration are less pleasant. Both can be utilized. The experience of fear, for example, gives us an opportunity to confront, acknowledge, and transform our boundaries. But when we feel love, we are powerful beyond measure. Those who are loved and love in return can accomplish any goal.

Future storytelling is one tool that was used to harness emotions. At a village fire or in a ritual, a future story would be told by a leader who hoped to accomplish great deeds or who had great hopes for the village. This powerful storyteller would fill the story of the future with detail and emotion. On the eve of a great battle, he might say:

> When I face our enemy I will feel fear, but I will remember that this fear is only to assist me in acting bravely and wisely. I will do this and I will conquer the enemy. Afterwards I will beam

with pride even though I will be exhausted, for I will know I have grown the fortune of our village, which I love, and we will all be joyous with the rewards the Sapa Inca will send us.

By telling the future story in this way, describing the details to fellow villages and stirring their emotions, a powerful group of energies were being brought to bear on co-creating this desired future.

Individual magic workers use this technique today. When one does a ritual or ceremony, prays, visualizes, or says affirmations, they include the emotions that accomplishing the desired results will bring. Many of the Incas knew that emotions are a side effect of human creation. We are spirit beings who volunteered to take on material bodies, leaving all our prebirth memories behind. On this planet where free will is a significant human factor, by blending spirit with material bodies you get emotions that spirits can seldom experience as human do.

Humanity is blessed with emotions, not a victim of them. We are not to be blown about by them without control, but rather we should become aware of and utilize the unique qualities of emotional energies to bring about a golden future! Become aware of your emotions; utilize them as powerful magical tools.

Finding Allies

Both the elders of a relocated village and their children in Cusco had to adapt and rise to their new life's challenges in order to survive and to help their village prosper. One of the best ways to do this was to make allies. The village elders who could overcome their prejudices and become friends with the elders of the new neighbor villages had a huge advantage. The princes who made friends with instructors or fellow students were most likely to rise to future positions of influence.

The Incan Empire did not forbid the worshipping of any Gods, Goddesses, or spiritual practices. The new citizens had to put the Incan Gods and Goddesses first, but they were usually allowed to keep their original beliefs, too. Thus, the village priests and shamans continued to perform their village's unique ceremonies. One of these, which was practiced widely, was the calling out and befriending of spiritual allies. These ceremonies are challenging for many modern-day people to imagine. We need to understand that there exist countless more living entities on Earth than our Western world acknowledges. We Westerners have placed blinders on our minds and don't often allow ourselves to see the true nature of existence and the countless magical entities that populate it.

The pre-Western Incas knew that there were spirit beings in nature and in other dimensions as well. They knew that these spirit beings would assist them if asked in the appropriate way. Spirit beings and potential allies come in countless forms and, because you live in the material world and you are contacting them, you always have control. Just what are spiritual allies? Well, the Irish have Leprechauns and banshees, the Hawaiians have Menehunes, and the Voodoo practitioners become possessed by their Loas or very indulgent Gods. I have met shamans who have received answers and great teachings from the fire spirits. These are all great examples of potential allies. I have as allies the spirits of llamas, dragonflies, pine trees, and some other entities that are beyond description.

You need to keep your mind open to call or find or even perceive allies. If you allow yourself to just accept that perhaps there are many forces and entities that are just waiting to manifest and assist you, then you can begin to imagine what they might be like and what they might be offering you.

Many people are more comfortable with terms such as guardian angels or spirit guides. These are forms of allies that can be effectively called upon for magical assistance. Some people at this point become fearful of devils, demons, ghosts, or evil forces taking them over. You must always remember that you are in control.

Fear is the only potential power that negative allies have over you. If you call, and a dark-side ally answers, tell it to get lost. Bad, selfish, or mischievous allies exist and can be utilized magically but should be repelled and not entertained by new students. The only power they can have over you is your fear or your bad intentions. Banish these, and you can call wonderful positive forces to your assistance.

When I can't file my papers, I call on some friendly allies to assist me, and they often do. When I am confused, I ask the wind for answers and clarity, and it usually comes. When I am overwhelmed, I hug a pine tree and become recharged. The best tools of all are your beliefs, imagination, and time.

There are in-depth rituals to call specific allies. However, for beginners I suggest that you sit by a fire, a candle, a stream, or at sunrise, sunset, or midnight and focus on calling an ally. Then, just let your imagination flow freely. Again, at first you might think you are making it up; go with that and trust in your power of creative imagination. In time it will change until your personal allies make it clear to you they do exist, and they can give you assistance and insights you could never get on your own.

Accessing Other Dimensions

Our planet Earth is a material world. The Incas were aware that there exist many more realms of existence than just the material. We use our five senses to see, feel, smell, hear, and taste our material world. Our sixth sense and our intuition are things that our material world today give little credence to. Yet we know that X-rays, ultraviolet rays, radio, TV, and magnetic rays all exist, even though we can't detect them with our five senses. To view the world as a collection of static, limited, and material places is not only wrong, it stifles all existence. The ancient Incas knew that there were many realms undetectable with normal human senses. That is how they learned to communicate with their Gods and Goddesses, the spirits of nature and animals, the mountains, and the wind itself. The shamans, healers, and elders attempted to translate these concepts to the conquering Spanish. The attempts at talking to these greedy conquistadors and fanatical Catholic priests about the importance of dimensional doorways was unsuccessful at best. The concepts translated poorly and were mostly condemned as pagan beliefs.

Approximately 95 percent of our brain power is either underutilized or not used at all. How can we begin to access more of its potential? Humans have an awe-inspiring system of sensory organs that most civilized people today seldom, if ever, utilize.

We have an aura, an ethereal body, an astral spirit, and seven chakras. An aura is the many leveled, multi-colored egg of energy that surrounds every living being and is visible to intuitives. It reflects your health and life story. The ethereal body is a spiritual double that exists for each of us. Strong spiritual people can cause these to appear elsewhere from their physical bodies. An example of this would be the resurrection of Christ, when his disciples reported seeing and speaking with him. Astral spirit is your dream body, which can be trained to separate from our sleeping physical body and fly anywhere on Earth or to other dimensions and bring back memories. The seven chakras are the energy centers that, again, are visible to inituitives, and control our health and well being. The first is at the base of your spine, and it controls survival. The second is located at your sexual organ and controls passion. The third is found above your belly button and controls your energy and balance. The fourth is your heart, your most powerful because it controls your ability to love. The fifth is in your throat and it controls communication. The sixth is above the center of your eyebrows and it controls your intuitive abilities. The seventh is found at the top of your head and it is your connection to the divine creative force. With attention to these aspects of our total being, we can learn to sense or even know things we can't logically see with the limitations we assign to our human bodies. Using our astral spirits or remote viewing (seeing things that are far away in your mind), we can also train ourselves to not only visit any place on Earth, but other dimensions as well.

Learning these skills takes belief, self-awareness, focused intent, and practice. As with realigning your life vision, astral traveling to other dimensions and bringing back clear memories is a matter of setting aside uninterrupted time and practicing patiently until you begin to succeed. The main requirement is fully believing that it can be done and that you can do it.

The Incan shamans would utilize these abilities in various ways to collect knowledge for all kinds of magical purposes. You too can do this. Simply stated, the best way to achieve astral travel is to have time away from your normal life. Reserve a nice period of time to dedicate completely to achieving "lift off." It is advantageous to fast in preparation and also to be well rested. Then lie down in a quiet, undisturbed place, and imagine your astral body floating out of your physical body. This may not occur on the first few attempts. However, with repeated effort you will achieve astral travel.

For those of you who want to astral travel but don't have much time, you can tell yourself as you fall asleep each night that you will astral travel in your dreams. If you visualize pulling your astral self out of your body by tugging on a rope as you fall asleep, this is often effective.

Adaptability

The Incas were fierce warriors. They conquered the area from Cusco to the middle of Chile, north to the middle of Ecuador, into Bolivia, and all the way to the Amazon jungle. They overcame all odds and established a cohesive Empire wherein all citizens were fed, clothed, and had homes. There existed many in-depth techniques for training warriors. However, for the modern-day Inca, adaptability is one of the most important.

Too many people sit around saying, "I was never given a chance," or "I was almost famous but this or that got in my way." There are numerous excuses for not living a fulfilling, joyous, powerful, meaningful, and passionate life. Well, if the universe hands you lemons, then figure out how to make the best lemonade available. If your entire being is committed to achieving goals, then whatever happens in your life, good or bad, can be seen as a wonderful opportunity to adapt and grow by overcoming this new setback or even turning it to your advantage.

A warrior doesn't say, "That village is too strategically placed to conquer." Rather they say, "We have never conquered a village so strategically placed; when we conquer this one, our unique victories will be spoken of at campfires throughout the Empire." So must your view be of all things as a modern Inca. Don't say that something can't be done just because you've never done it before. Rather, make concrete plans and go forth with focused intent, clear vision, and passion, and boldly pursue your dreams! How wonderful it will be when you have accomplished what you set out to do against all odds. Now you are on the magical path toward growth and evolution as a modern Inca.

4

Thinking of the Incas

Journal Entry—October 11, 2001: *We are settled down*
here in Cusco. Having seen Lima, Macchu Pichu, and the
Amazon, the next step of our plan called for finding a nice yet
reasonably priced apartment in Cusco, which we could use as
our home base for the next month or two. We have recently
connected with some old friends from San Francisco. Tim and
Betty along with their eleven-year-old daughter Mila, and their
nine-year-old son, Joaquin, who have been living here for the
past year. They are involved with a Cusco-based weaving coop-
erative whose mission is to keep alive the ancient weaving tra-
ditions of the villages. It will be great having them here.

We spent the last two days searching for an apartment. The
four of us walked from one end of town to the other, looking at
rentals that people had told us about, homes that were adver-
tised in the newspaper, or places which just had signs out. We
followed our every lead and instinct, hoping to find a furnished
apartment with at least two bedrooms that isn't too cramped or
expensive. Despite our very best efforts, we didn't find any-
thing appropriate on the first day.

Well into our second day of stalking around Cusco, I was
beginning to consider lowering my standards and renting a
place the rest of the family didn't like. Sophia stated that the
whole process made her feel insecure and sad. She felt that this
is how poor and homeless people must feel, drifting around in
hopes of finding something better but just experiencing one dis-
appointment after another.

As the sun began to set, we found ourselves on Chochquecha
Street, just three blocks away from the central Plaza de Armas.
Henry saw a "For Rent" sign at a building named Hostel
Central. We knocked and an energetic woman answered the

door. We later found out that her name was Luz; she told us that they had vacant, furnished apartments which rented by the month. She went and got the owner, a Señor Ruben Chavez, who also seemed very open and friendly. Together, they showed us a lovely apartment with a wonderful view of the city, a balcony, and pretty much everything else we were hoping for, except no refrigerator. It turns out refrigerators aren't used much in Cusco. We were rather concerned about the price, but when we asked, the rent was within our reasonable range.

We signed the rental agreement, gave Señor Chavez our deposit, and will move in tomorrow morning. Wow! We successfully found our dream apartment in Cusco. It is fascinating to place your fate in the hands of destiny. The universe has happily conspired to bless us at this particular moment in time, here in the land of my children and the ancient Incas.

One of the gladdest moments in human life, methinks, is the departure upon a distant journey to unknown lands. Shaking off with one mighty effort the fetters of habit, the leaden weight of routine, the clock of many cares, and the slavery of home, man feels once more happy. The blood flows with the fast circulation of childhood . . . afresh draws the morning of life.

—Sir Richard Burton, Journal Entry
December 2nd, 1957

Visualization and Goal Setting

Seemingly impossible goals often can be reached through faith and visualization. Despite many obstacles, my family and I returned to Peru in the fall of 2001. We were last here together in 1990, when we first became a family. At that time, my wife and I promised ourselves that we would bring the children back to spend a prolonged period of time in Peru before they became teenagers. Well, we missed by a year. Henry Miguel turned 13 in August 2001. Sophia Zila turned 12 the day before. We realized last summer that it was time to act, for if we waited any longer we would be dragging two mature teenagers all over Peru. The teenage years tend to be difficult, and Peru tends to be challenging. The combination seemed daunting; we were highly motivated to take action without further delay.

Once we agreed that our trip would occur in the fall, it was as if the Incan Gods and Goddesses cleared the obstacles and put an amazing sequence of events in place to allow us to spend the last four months of the year in Peru. Pulling the children out of school and arranging to do home schooling while traveling proved the least of our challenges. My wife applied for a leave from the university at which she is employed, and beat the odds in getting one. She is using this time to write a book about the importance of the native culture to children who are adopted from other countries, how this affects their lives, and the affect that returning to their homeland may have on them. Meanwhile, I was blessed to be able to bring together a highly qualified management team to run *Magical Blend* magazine and MB Media in my absence. Just before our departure, I had a drink at the cafe across the street from our MB Media office and bid the staff adieu for four months. I am truly blessed to work with wonderful, talented, and creative people of such high ideals. It is also a blessing to be able to trust this team to run the magazines and the business in my absence. This will be one of only three times in the past 24 years that I have been away from MB Media for a month or more.

America and Peru

My family and I have already seen and shared so much in Peru! It is mind boggling what you can fit into your life when you take out business, school, responsibilities, and all the other tired habits of the workaday world. In spite of all our varied experiences and adventures, we barely scratched the surface of Peru. You could spend lifetimes traveling and studying in the Andes and the Amazon and not even begin to get the true essence of the wonders, the mysteries, and the splendor of what is and was there. My children missed junior high, sports, electronics, and their friends, yet they enjoyed Peru immensely. I am amazed and impressed by their adaptability and enthusiasm. For my wife and I, the trip was something like a second honeymoon. We didn't lose our tempers very much and found ourselves to be more forgiving with one another and the children. We laughed and cuddled more. She kept saying how much she loved Peru.

Back in the 1960s, Simon and Garfunkel wrote words to the ancient Incan song named "El Condor Pasa." The lyrics say, "I would rather be a hammer than a nail. Yes I would, if I only could." That is how Peru has made me feel. I want to shake and wake the world to the beauty of existence, and to our ability to appreciate and increase that beauty.

Our apartment in Cusco was a short five-minute walk to the Plaza de Armas. Our street was a dead end, with the Imperial bus stop on the corner. Our neighbors were a mix of tourists, expatriots and local people. Fruit stands and neighborhood shops and cafes punctuated the residential buildings. Many llamas, burros, and sheep paraded up and down our street each day, mostly for tourist pictures but a grand sight nonetheless. The simplicity and beauty of the time we spent there is some thing that I will never forget.

A Rainy Night in Cusco

One rainy evening, I went out alone for a walk. To get to the plaza, I turned left down Calle Hatunruimiyoc, where no cars can drive. I passed an elderly native woman, who had a blue plastic tarp wrapped tightly around herself and the souvenirs she had for sale. Her hair was of course dark black and braided down her back. She smiled at me and held up a damp baby's sweater. "Papaicito chompa," she said.

"No gracias," I replied, with a tight smile. Her eyes glinted and I felt moved by her struggle to make ends meet.

I tightened up my poncho and pulled down my hat because the wind was blowing the rain down my neck. There were not many salespeople about. The shoeshine boys and postcard sellers were all home hiding from the rain. Just a stray tourist and an occasional local walked by, attempting to stay warm and dry. I stopped to appreciate the Incan stone wall that lines this street. How was this stone cut so precisely and fit together so securely without mortar? You can feel its antiquity. The stones themselves seem alive. I fantasized that these stones act as guardians of Peru, that they actually flow as a river when they want to. I seemed to hear them on some telepathic level. They tell me that they are awaiting the pre-arranged ancient signal, and when it is given, they will rise up and crush the greedy and selfish. The ancient Incan stonework will return Peru to the innocent, hard-working Quechuen people.

This trip to Peru with my family caused me to be very thankful for my life. It also permitted me to see how much the world missed out by having the Incan culture marginalized by Spanish and Western influences. The Incan culture had—and in some ways, more than ever still has—much to offer the world in terms of art, vision, values, and love. And, of course, ritual and magic, too.

5

Incan Rituals

Journal Entry—October 23, 2001: *Ritual is important to all cultures, at all times. Life itself is a ritual. Coming to Peru with my family was something I had hoped to do for over a decade. In all that time of hoping and planning, I never imagined that the trip itself would be a ritual of sorts for my children. If they had lived here in the time of the Incas, Sophia might now, at the age of 12, be selected as a Virgin of the Sun. At 13, Henry would be undergoing his ritual of initiation into manhood. Instead, over the next several years, they will be coming of age in the United States of the twenty-first century.*

Deborah and I have remarked often that Sophia and Henry have changed a great deal in the last few years. That's normal, of course. But the changes that they will experience in the coming years will make all that seem minimal by comparison. We hope that this trip will help build the foundation and provide them the touchstones that will get us through their teenage years together. No matter how they grow and mature, the four of us will always have this intimate four-month period to remember with love and affection.

Rites of passage were very important to the Incas. Our days in Peru represent a rite of passage for my entire family, but especially for Sophia and Henry. Before we left the United States, they both held a mixed jumble of images and ideas of what Peru was really like. Being here now, for this lengthy period of time, permits them to see the reality of Peru. They have seen its poverty and its wonders. They have come to know how friendly and open the Peruvian people are. They have gone from being confused about what it meant to

be Peruvian to being excited and proud of their magnificent
heritage.

I could not have asked for a better rite of passage for my
children.

Background of Incan Rituals

The Incan society was highly ritualistic. They believed
that ceremonies and rituals kept them connected to the
divine forces surrounding them. Today in rural Peru, the
Quechuen descendants of the Incas still have ceremonies
and rituals for most occasions. In Cusco, fireworks are
shot off almost every morning in honor of one saint or
another. It seems more days than not there are parades
honoring those saints in the Plaza de Armas.

Ritual takes many forms. In all of them, the most
important elements are belief, intent, desire, expectation,
creativity, and interpretation. Rituals have existed
throughout history. They are either a way to enlist the
help of the deities or they are a way to alter reality to better suit the performers' desires. Simply put, a ritual is
what you make it. My experiences have taught me that
rituals are as powerful and as effective as your studies
and practice can make them.

The subject of rituals elicits strong opinions in Peru
today. There are those critics who feel that the old rituals
should be performed in precisely the same manner that
they have been for centuries. These critics feel that
shamans and healers who instruct Westerners are altering
and trivializing the traditions of their ancestors. I, on the
other hand, feel that the traditions, rituals, and ceremonies
of the Incas and their ancestors are living traditions

that have evolved for centuries. To me and others who believe as I do, these rituals are most alive and meaningful when they are undergoing this kind of evolution. They were meant to be modified with time, not frozen in some unchangeable and, for modern practitioners, unrecognizable form. It is undeniable that these ways changed and adapted when the Incas conquered new regions. They changed and evolved again when the Christians came. Today they are changing and evolving from the Western influence.

I feel strongly that the best Incan shamans, healers, and priests of today or of the past are and were the best actors. There is a strong school of thought that says that, if you have not descended or been initiated by an Andean holy person or healer, then you cannot become one. I strongly disagree. I feel that a healer, shaman, or holy person must be judged on their own merits. If they do good works and achieve results, it doesn't matter who they are or how they came by their skills. I realize that there is something lost and something gained in both schools of thought. I have stated my strong opinion here. If you don't feel spiritually capable of performing an effective ritual, do it anyway. Act as if you are a God or Goddess and you will soon have such experiences you will no longer have to act.

Clarity of purpose and intensity of intent and will are more important than form and detail in most rituals. The Incas were always building on and borrowing from some unimaginably magnificent pre-Incan cultures. This is how they built their awesome Empire: by adapting the best of what had come before them.

Ritual is still central to Peruvian existence. Inti Rayman, the celebration of Peru's winter Solstice, celebrated in June each year (their winter is summer in the U.S.), has become as world famous as Mardi Gras. The

Incas used to bring out the bodies of all the Sapa Incas and parade them around, but the Spanish brought a stop to that. However, the old Sapa Incas never really died. They were brought out in the plaza for all big festivals. Shamans, priests, and members of the nobility solicited their advice. Those who are especially sensitive can still feel their spirits in Cusco.

Beyond the Sapa Incas, every person in every village had their own rituals of life. They prayed to their Gods, ancestors, and nature spirits for guidance and help. They gave offerings to many spiritual entities to keep them happy and stay in their good graces. Chicha, a traditional beer made from corn, was used as sacrificial material for the Gods and Goddesses far more often than blood.

Incan rituals as practiced by the priests were very different from those practiced by the shamans. The priests and priestesses usually practiced rituals to keep the Gods happy and to enlist their aid for the Sapa Incas and the Empire.

The shamans and *curendarios* (traditional healers) were not bound by state traditions or a huge religious organization. When the Catholic Church destroyed most Incan temples and idols in large numbers, *curandarios*, shaman healers, and *brujos* (what we might call a witch or magic worker) filled in the gaps with tales, effective healing techniques, and rituals in every village and city in the Andes.

Reality-altering rituals, which combined vision, will, and intent, were well-known to both the priests and the shamans. However, then as now, only those who dared to cross the dimensional doorways and dance in the dark corners where insanity often lurks were able to accomplish these rituals. The Incas had rituals for raising the spirits of the dead, for calling spirits to serve them, for changing weather patterns, for attracting lovers, for increasing or decreasing fertility. The Catholic Church believed these rituals to be evil and the domain of the devil. Thus, many have been hidden for over 400 years.

There are many stories, legends, and myths that say the Incas knew in advance of the coming Spanish conquest. These stories often go on to say how the most important treasures were taken from the temples and hidden until the time was right for their return. Some stories have them thrown into lakes, especially Lake Titicaca. Others say that these priceless artifacts are hidden underground or in caves. There are even stories told about treasures in a tunnel under Cusco. One such story tells of three intrepid souls who attempted to explore the tunnel in 1890. The three explorers were in the tunnel for three days. Only one stumbled out, bringing with him a golden ear of corn and a fantastic tale of demons killing his colleagues. After this, the city and Peruvian governments chose to take no chances; they used explosives to block the cave entrances and then hid them in an attempt to prevent future loss of lives. Today, with the blessings of the Peruvian government, the Catholic Church, and the city of Cusco, the Boric Ruz Explorer Organization and the University of Lima are presently using sonar and electromagnetic instruments to search these tunnels for possible treasures. Their searching has already revealed two previously undiscovered ancient Incan mummies. If there truly are lost Incan treasures in tunnels under Cusco, a city where more than 360,000 tourists visit from all over the world each year, then what treasures might remain hidden in remote caves, lakes, and valleys, or even in the Amazon jungle itself?

The stories of hidden treasures are just the tip of the iceberg. There are also the tales of the huge, golden disk of the sun that is said to have hung in Cusco's Sun Temple, Coraconcha. According to the legends, the first

Inca, Manco Capa, brought this fabulous disk to the Empire. Spanish documents indicate that a disk was indeed spirited away from Cusco by the conquistadors. Another disk, said to be one and the same, was found in the once lost city of Vilcabamba and sent to King Philip with the message that he should send it on to the Pope because it had fantastic spiritual and miraculous properties. Where is this disk today? No one seems to know for sure, but it wouldn't be out of character for the imperial Spaniards to have melted it down out of greed. Other legends state that the disk sent to Spain was merely a lesser replica, and that the original was taken to the shores of Lake Titicaca. There, shamans and priests opened an inter-dimensional doorway, where the disk was transported to another plane of existence. There it will remain safe and out of the hands of evildoers until the planet and its people are ready for its return.

I have good reasons to believe that other dimensions exist, and that knowledge and material items can be hidden in them. Of course, often the best place to hide something is in the most obvious place. If something is right under your nose you seldom really see it. It is like that with a great deal of knowledge in Peru. Much of it is available in the isolated villages by talking with the people after you earn their trust. They are available from the old and crippled beggars who are on the streets of each major city. The meek are often the most powerful. First you must learn how to see; then you must learn how to ask; finally, you must learn how to safely use these ancient rituals in today's world.

I have some knowledge of rites and rituals, which I feel is relatively safe and approachable for those who will read this book. More will be revealed in time. As you seek so shall you find. As you evolve, you will find yourself able to handle more, and more complicated, rituals.

Magical Rituals

In the Incan way of life, so much is dictated by tradition that a great deal becomes ritualized almost by rote. However, personal discrimination is required to decide between rituals that are convenient habits, those that are just show, and those that are meaningful, and even powerful, in their proper execution.

There are numerous traditional rituals. Among the rituals for healers, there are many varied harvest rituals that are both powerful and precise, because you must follow every detail exactly if you hope to harvest effective cures. The rituals of the Incan healers and shamans are rarely shared in complete detail with Westerners. We Westerners are believed by many magic workers of the Andes to be the ones who will resurrect the old ways and save the future through them. However, these shamans usually omit details in training, apparently so that we can rediscover or recreate them for ourselves.

I have spoken with keepers of the powerful holy ancient ways and rituals. I have been gifted with knowledge by more than a few. This knowledge is firmly rooted in the oral tradition, however, I will share them in a written format to the best of my ability.

Many spiritual Incas knew of many things that existed on the planet Earth far beyond the shores of South America in their day and even into the future. They knew of these things from their astral travels. These spiritual Incas chose not to bring these things into the Empire because they saw the long-range picture. They grieved in advance for the end of the Empire and the fact that their way of life would end. Yet, they knew that after its pain-filled ending, their culture would rise again like a phoenix from the ashes of both the Incan Empire and the Western civilization that would follow. They knew that one day the best of the Incan ways would be resurrected and bring forward the best that planet Earth and humanity have to share. So they allowed everything that has happened in the last five hundred years to happen, for the good of the future, and for the amazingly powerful effect the Incan way of life and knowledge would eventually have on all of us. Rituals should often include the elements and the spirits of the main directions or, as the Incas referred to them, the four quadrants: North, South, East, and West. Rituals often call on the spirits from places of power. Any benevolent entities that the person performing the ritual feels passionately about may be evoked. Just use caution and progress slowly.

Creating a Reservoir for Your Magical Energies

There is a less intense yet equally powerful ritual I have performed with great success, and you can, too. Choose a magical item. It can be a wooden staff, a bowl, a knife, a rock, a crystal, or a gem—almost any item will do. It must be something that will endure through time. A candle will not do, nor will sea salt or incense. This item must be something you can develop a strong emotional attachment to and something you see as able to hold magical energies. Once you have chosen this tool, sit with it alone. Call in a simple ritual to the most powerful, highest spiritual beings in which you believe. Ask them to purify this tool and to empty it of its past energies. Then wash it in sea salt water. Dry it, and burn sage around it. Now imagine that all your passions, hopes, and love are pouring into it. Say:

> I name this magical tool as the reservoir of my magical energies. Every time I perform a ritual I will use this tool, and it will become more powerful and blessed until the day that it can give power back to me or the one I give it to. May the

magic of the Incas, the Andes Mountains, and my truest essences make this so.

Then, each time you do a ritual, handle, use, and charge this tool. When you are not using it, keep it wrapped in a dark cloth and whenever possible, store it in the same special place. Eventually you will feel it radiating power and energy. It will add effectiveness to your rituals. When my children had their rites of passage, I gifted them both with magical tools I had ritualistically charged in this way. They both use them and cherish them and they know a part of me is in their special tool.

Passing Down the Traditions of Shamanic Energies

Rituals can be used to direct your will and store your intense passionate energies, for yourself or another to draw on at any time. There was a special ritual among the shamans of some regions of the Incan Empire. A piece of gold or silver or a gem or crystal was radiated with an elder shaman's energies and passions. When the elder felt his death approaching, he would make a deep cut in the arm of his apprentice. Into the open wound he would place the sacred object that radiated his power and passions. Then he would sew up the wound with ritually blessed llama gut thread, performing the ritual of the passage of power. The young shaman would always bless and energize this embedded magical talisman during every ritual he performed. As he, too, aged and his death grew close, he would cut it out of its long-healed wound and implant it in his apprentice, performing again the ritual of the passage of power. In this way, the energies of the past shamans were always present, and future rituals would be enhanced by the power of the past.

Rites of Initiation

In the Incan Empire there were ceremonies of passage when people reached certain stages in their lives. They were called Rites of Initiation. Among those marked stages were reaching adulthood, getting married, and becoming an elder.

Each spring in ancient Cusco, on the vernal equinox, all the boys who had turned thirteen in the past year would gather in front of Coraconcha, the Temple of the Sun. The priests would throw the ashes of the winters' sacrifices into the river. As they tumbled down the valley, the boys would run to keep pace with the ashes. They would race this way, ten miles to the south, where their families would be waiting for them with a sacred meal to refresh them before the sprint back to Cusco. This signified the beginning of a full year of initiation for these boys, who would be tested to prove their worth throughout the next twelve months.

The ceremony involved in becoming an elder was similar to many other shamanic initiation rites. When a person had lived longer than most of the others in his or her village and was no longer of great assistance in labor, he or she were initiated as an elder. This was a symbolic ritual in which the initiate passed out of normal life, faced the inevitability of their death, and pledged to assist the village leaders in making wise decisions based on their experience and the knowledge of what had been attempted in the past.

After initiation, the elders did little physical labor. They were honored and fed by the village as the ones who had been chosen by the Gods to live long and grow wise. Their opinions and decisions could only be overruled by the Sapa Inca, other royalty, the priests, or the Cusco-trained village leaders. However, most leaders and people in positions who could overturn the elders' decisions were wise enough to act on the elders' advice.

There were other initiations. One of the most important occurred when the most beautiful girls were selected to be Virgins of the Sun. They were sworn in and made to pledge that their old lives were ashes, and their new lives were solely to serve the God Inti, the Sapa Inca, and their specified representatives.

Young boys who were chosen by the village shaman for the priesthood were similarly initiated. They were no longer who they had been; they were now symbolically killed and resurrected as focused and rededicated individuals. These Incan priests participated in ceremonies and rituals that were said to have come from the first Incas. Their ceremonies were performed in order to produce harmony, consistency, and loyalty throughout the empire as well as to gain the blessings of the Sapa Incas and the Gods and Goddesses. In contrast, the shamans, healers, and other magic workers and their traditions varied greatly from region to region and village to village. The more effective ones had broken the codes of nature and understood many of the mysteries of existence. They could astral travel long distances not only on Earth, but also in other dimensions. They could effect the future and aid in the continued prosperity of their village.

Shamanic Initiation Rituals

Initiation rituals were and are used to mark new beginnings or passages from one stage of life to another. The initiations from region to region and village to village varied. Often, the boys who were to become shamans were made to suffer by fasting, strenuous exercise, ritual, or even mind-altering herbs such as San Padro

Catcus or Ayahuasca. Whichever path was used, the goal was for them to experience a form of death, and their spirit to go off on its own adventuring. While in the other realms, dimensions, or astral planes, they established the personal reference points that are the only reliable maps in these realms. When they returned and recovered, they had experienced existence beyond the material plane. They now had the ability to go back to those places, either on behalf of others or in search of additional wisdom.

Today there are many ways to recreate the shamanic initiation. The best is for you to create your own personalized rite of passage. Make it your own. Use your intuition. Never risk real death, but do cut the connection with your normal life and the physical world. More than once I have fasted for two weeks while backpacking alone in the mountains. I left information of my planned route and instructions with a friend if I was not at a rendezvous point by a certain day. Then they and others had instructions where to come looking for me. While hiking, I prayed for guidance and transformative experiences. I tried to avoid sleeping at night. Rather, I would sit with my back to a tree facing a fire and pray.

Usually at some point, always a different number of days out, I would have an experience. It might be a vision, disembodied voices, astral traveling, or just falling asleep and having otherworldly dreams. This is just one method. If you choose to undergo a ritual of initiation, be creative, use your intuition, trust your inner guidance, but inform friends of your plans just to be safe.

True shamanic wisdom comes in many bizarre forms, and the secret to using it to enrich your life is being open with the contradictions they cause. You must also trust your insights and inner guidance to translate what happened and what it added to your knowledge.

Gathering Incan Ceremonial Tools

If you have decided to walk the path of the modern Inca, then you will have to choose a new self-definition. Are you someone who could become an Incan shaman or healer, or even an Incan elder? If so, then you will need to gather your tools for the Incan field of your choice and discover the way you are guided to craft them. Tools come in countless forms. They can be purely symbolic, as with a ceremonial knife, or they can be practical, as with a healer's rare herbs.

The gathering of Incan tools and the learning of your Incan craft are matters of trust, trial, and error, inner knowing, and research. If you are drawn to the healer path, you must study and then learn to communicate with plants and the human body. If you are drawn to become an Incan shaman, healer, or elder, you will need a ceremonial altar. You will also need a number of magical tools for everything from cutting your ties to the material world, to gathering psychic energies, to preparing stews and magical tinctures.

Most people who choose to take control of their lives need to make the collection of wisdom a goal. It is especially true that elders need wisdom. Wisdom is a tool that can only be developed over time with focused intent. It is not to be confused with knowledge. Knowledge is gathering information and facts. Wisdom is learning how the universe works and how to better assist it in moving as you desire. If you pray, do so with the clear intent of becoming wiser. Wisdom doesn't usually come to those who do not work to develop it. The goal for those who choose the modern Incan path is to recreate the grand techniques, skills, and insights that allowed a poor mountain tribe to rule an empire larger than the Roman Empire.

Incan Ceremonial Tools

A person can find extremely effective ceremonial tools almost anywhere. The main ingredients for success are to be clear about what you are hoping to achieve with the tools and how you are likely to use them. I was fortunate enough to acquire most of my magical tools in Peru, but that is not a requirement. Decide which tools you want to start with, and then begin to stalk them. Let intuition and imagination be your guide.

Of course, you can always go to a metaphysical store and purchase these tools. Alternatively, you can search online for magical supplies or Peruvian imports. I honestly feel that most of these are overpriced, and if you find your own tools around your home or in second-hand stores you are much better off. If you decide to purchase your tools, bear in mind that there exists an ancient Incan belief that they will lose their power if bargained for. If you decide you want a magical tool you see in a store, simply ask the price and either pay it or look elsewhere. To make a counteroffer creates energy stating that this tool may be of lesser value. You want tools that are of highest value!

Whatever you take home as a ceremonial tool must be cleansed. To do this, you can perform the following small ceremony. First, call on the four directions to realign its energies. Then ask Inti to burn out all impurities, ask Pacha Mama to make it fertile and brand new, and ask Pacsa Mama to fill it with the power of the unseen. Rinse the object thoroughly in salt water. While you are doing this, repeat, "I remove your past and give you a new life." Then dry it with a clean cloth and burn coca leaves or sage around it. Move the smoke about it preferably which a feather from a condor, however, any type of bird's feather will do. Say, "This smoke cleanses all impurities and raises your vibrations to the highest spiritual level. My magical work and ceremonies will always be positive and effective for the highest good of all concerned."

This done, your tool is ready to use. When not in use, and provided that your altar is in a safe and relatively private place, you may leave it set up and the tools laying on it. If not, then wrap them in a clean cloth, pillow case, or sheet and place them in a secure closet or drawer away from other probing energies.

List of Incan Ceremonial Tools

Usable athema or kuchuna: some form of sharp object used for cutting

Reservoir athema or kuchuna: a sharpened condor or llama bone.

Kuchuna: ritual cloth

Unkuna: a ceremonial shawl preferable made of hand woven wool from llama, alpaca, or vicuna

Altar: a table, overturned box, or any flat surface that can be transported

Hatumpi ccatu or despacho: offerings to the Gods

Ara: firestone, to build your offering fire on

Mismarumi: a sandstone representing the celebrants

Mama ccocha: a marine shell to hold alcohol or wine

Humihua: a narrow-necked container for water

Magical staff or wand

Herbs: coca, sage, others as needed

Illa: llama charm

Ritual flute, whistle, Zamponas or Pan pipes

Clay water vessel

Condor, toucan, or parrot feather

Salt: preferably sea salt from Peru

Ceremonial candles
Semiprecious gems or crystals
Vegetables: potatoes and corn, others as appropriate

Incan Ceremonial Tools Explained

Usable Athema or Kuchuna

A recent dig on the shores of Lake Titicaca found ritual-istic needles and knifes carved from delicate condor bones. Llama bones also make great ceremonial knives, as will almost any bones. Of course, you just need a sharp instrument for both symbolic and real cutting.

Reservoir Athema or Kuchuna

This can be anything to which you have an emotional attachment, and that you can put aside to only be used for your rituals. The Incas often used a rock from the highest peak they had climbed. When my horse died I cut hair from her mane and this became the reservoir of the spiritual, psychic, and other dimensional energies generated in my rituals.

Kuchuna Ritual Cloth

This cloth represents the four quarters of the universe. Turning first north, then east, west, and south is of major significance in most Incan ritual. You should have a rit-ual cloth with black in the north or upper left quadrant, fading to brown in the south or lower right, then to gray in the upper right or east, altering slowly to white in the lower left, west. It is best if this cloth is handwoven in

Peru from natural llama or alpaca wool and colored with natural Peruvian dyes. It is even better if your cloth is created by an elder weaver who understands how to fill it with spiritual possibilities. However, at the other extreme, you can hand dye two- to three-foot square cloths yourself or sew together four squares of dyed cloth. This cloth can be used as a shawl or an altar cloth on which you can place your other magical instruments. In truth any cloth cleansed and rededicated exclusively for ritual will suffice.

Hatumpi Ccatu or Despacho

If you travel to Peru or almost any other Latin American country, you can visit an Andean medical shop or curandero supply stand and purchase an offering package known as a *despacho*. In Peru, Ecuador, and Bolivia, these items are premade for certain Gods, or you may just purchase the individual items.

Illa

This is a charmed amulet used as a figurine or drawing, or even on a matchbox, often in the shape of a llama. Before the Spanish came, two illa were placed on every rooftop to carry prayers to the Gods and receive blessings in return.

Unkuna

This ceremonial shawl assists the practitioner who wants to have a foot in the material world and a foot in the spiritual dimensions. Another way to say that is to have your body on Earth and your spirit soaring in the Heavens. The Unkuna, when placed on your shoulders, brings spiritual energies into you. I prefer a handwoven llama, alpaca, vicuna, or wool manta. However some people prefer a woven poncho or a even a cape or kind of priest's habit. The point is to have a magical garment that is only used in ceremony. A specially dedicated bathrobe can work just fine.

Ara

This is a large stone on which you can build your offering fire. I did not bring one back from Peru, because they are generally quite heavy. What you want if you are planning to perform ceremonies outside is a flat large rock on which you can build your fire. It is best to use one that you have ritually blessed and spiritually cleansed for all your ceremonies. However, it is fine to bless one anew when in a new or different location. Indoors I use an old camping Dutch-oven cooking pot that I have blessed for this purpose and that will safely hold heat.

Mismarumi

Standing stones or small pebbles representing the celebrants are a nice addition to any ritual. I have four or five stones found in different special locations. If I have more participants, I find and consecrate more stones. Usually I just rededicate each stone to a different celebrant each time. The Incas believed whatever was done in the material world also was mirrored in the spiritual realms. These rocks can become symbolic participants in your ceremonies.

Mama Ccocha

This is a marine shell to hold alcohol or wine. In Peru, conch shells were preferred. In California, abalone shells will work. Even a clam or mussel shell will suffice. It just needs to be a shell from a water creature, which will hold alcohol to represent the rivers, lakes, and oceans.

Humihua

This is a narrow-necked container for water. The Incan shamans had these specially made for this one use. You can still purchase them in certain Latin American markets, but any vase with a narrow neck is an acceptable replacement. The narrow neck represents the passage of the spiritual energies from Earth to the other dimensions and back. Only those energies that are the most adaptable will successfully get through.

Magical Staff or Wand

This is an extension of your material being. With this wand, you can extend your energies beyond normal reach. There is almost no limit to the effectiveness of your intent and spiritual energies when properly refined and extended in this manner. My own experience in finding a magical staff was quite illuminating. I'll tell you the story shortly.

Magical or Healing Herbs

All substances of nature should be harvested with great care. Herbs are very powerful substances and should only be taken under the guidance of someone very experienced and trained in these skills. Start small with an easy guidebook and the local health food store supplies. The in-depth esoteric concoctions should be only a possible long-range goal.

The coca leaves are important to Incan ritual, however, fill-ins may be used. These include sage, bay leaves, chamomile, and others as your imagination suggests. Good replacements can be purchased in markets and health-food stores or harvested in the wild. Coca leaves are preferred when available. Remember, however, that coca leaves are not legal in many countries.

Ritual Flute, Whistle, Zamponas, or Panpipes

In ritual work, music serves as a beautiful language of the Gods and Goddesses. Magical musical instruments can set the tone and attract the attention of spiritual entities.

Clay Water Vessel

As with the seashell, the purpose of this tool is to hold ritual liquids. Clay pottery is best because it is of the Earth. However, glass or metal can work. Your vessel should be the size and shape of a small bowl.

Condor, Toucan, or Parrot Feather

Birds fly closest to the divine energies. Exotic bird feathers like those listed work best to expand your imagination. However, chicken or pigeon feathers, if used properly, will raise the spiritual energies of the ceremony.

Salt

Life cannot exist without salt. It is preferable to use sea salt from Peru. Sea salt is closest to nature. Salt cleanses and expands possibilities.

Ceremonial Candles

I have purchased many magical candles in Peru. Some people prefer to make their own, but most any candle can work. It represents the light of life, hope, and expectations, carrying our ceremonies to the heavens.

Semiprecious Gems or Crystals

Quartz crystals grow and resonate directly from Pacha Mama. They focus and direct energies on a subatomic level. The Incas, as well as many other native peoples, knew this. Every mineral and gem has unique properties that can be tapped and utilized in ceremonies. I keep a wide array. As with herbs, do your own research and experiment freely; you'll be amazed at the various qualities of some magical crystals. Amethyst, as an example, is great for lessening substance abuse and attracting riches.

Vegetables

Pacha Mama gives us all life. Her fruits and vegetables sustain us. Potatoes and corn fed the Incan Empire and are the main staple of many Andean peoples today. Having vegetables, fruit, and flowers in your ceremonies connects you to the Earth and fertility. They are difficult to use for prolonged periods of time and must be replaced frequently. Just be sure that you clean and bless the new ones before each ceremony.

For any other tools you might require, be creative. Let your intuition, intent, and imagination be your only limits. I follow this with a story of how I began gathering my ceremonial tools. Let this story inspire and direct you.

My First Magical Staff

Soon after deciding to learn about becoming a shaman, I assumed that I needed a magical staff. I asked the spirits to provide direction toward the staff that was right for me. In shamanic work you have to develop an inner ability to receive true and positive guidance. I found myself drawn to a San Francisco city dumpster. "No! No! No! This can't be right!" I protested, yet the spirit seemed to be pushing me with some insistence. "OK! I'll climb in," I said, and climb in I did! Once in the dumpster, I saw lots of plasterboard and broken furniture. I wondered aloud, "Was a leg of a broken coffee table meant to be my magic staff? No. How about an old wall slat? No." They just didn't feel right. Remember, following your instincts is all-important in magic work.

Then I had another strange feeling to reach in a pile of junk. "Yeah, yeah, sure," I protested, fighting with myself. "I am taking this too far," I said out loud. "No, you're not! Now, do it now," urged my inner voice. So I did. I plunged my hand deep into the junk pile, cutting my skin on a broken lamp in the process. But then I felt what I thought was a dry branch. Pulling it out, I discovered that it was a large, dead houseplant with the roots still attached. I broke off the thickest branch and climbed out of the dumpster, thinking, "What a strange magical shaman's staff! And what a strange way to find it." As the weeks went by I painted my staff and tied feathers to it. It seemed to be absorbing my passion for life and a positive future. It never looked like an impressive magical staff, but it served perfectly for all the ceremonies I created.

A few months after I had found my staff, a friend of mine died of AIDS. When I heard the news, I performed the ceremony to assist his soul in its transition. A couple of days later, I picked up my magical wand and it was growing geranium leaves! I took it with me that day to the funeral and the cemetery. I went back after everyone left and planted my magic geranium staff on my friend's grave. The last time I visited the grave, the Geranium bush was huge. I am sure my unlikely magical staff helped his spirit's evolution and that it originally called to me for that purpose.

I suggest that you always let your inner voice be your guide in choosing tools or a spiritual path. You have access to all the knowledge in the universe. You just have to turn off your TV more and turn on your passion for personal growth. Then check that inner voice often to make sure it is guiding you well. It is okay if it seems silly or even confusing, but never let it take you to the dark side, into evil or dangerous places. Always remember: you have control and free will!

The Proper Energies

A person who has almost died from an accident, a medical condition, or a risky adventure usually lives differently then the rest of humanity. They always seem to be exerting extra intensity in pushing their personal

envelopes and living every day to the fullest. Their attitude is one of fun, of absence of fear, of saying, "Let's live
the moment to its fullest because we will never be in this
moment again and any of us could be dead at any
moment!" That to me is also the Incan way.

Then there is the element of the surreal. This is difficult to explain, especially as it relates to ritual. I am told
that most of the famous writers who have come out of
Peru were surrealists. But how else could you view reality if you grew up in Peru? In the United States, Europe,
and Japan, we strive to make life predictable and safe,
regular, and often boring. Are these the lives we want?

In Peru, the people have persisted and survived.
They have usually suffered tragedies both personal and
national in scope, yet still savored life and celebrated
when the occasions arose. Their weddings, baptisms, and
even birthday parties usually involve entire villages. At a
minimum, these celebrations last 24 hours or more and
include a great deal of dancing, singing, eating, storytelling, and drinking. They are a warm and sharing people, full of love for life and humanity. It is not a country
for the squeamish. Dirt, excrement (human and animal),
and safety hazards abound! In the United States, we feel
it is the responsibility of a hole to warn everyone of its
presence. In Peru, they feel that it is everyone's responsibility to know where the holes are and not fall or drive
into them. In the United States, we are fanatical about fin-
ishing touches. Things must look completed even if they
are not. In Peru, house are always being built or
enlarged. Electrical lights and wires dangle and spark.
For example, when we were in Peru, we rented a great
apartment with a lovely dining-room table. The tabletop
however, was never screwed on to the legs properly, it
wobbled dangerously. Oh well, live with it or fix it seem
to be the attitude of the landlord. Being North Americans

we went out, bought a screw driver and screws, flipped the table over, and made it secure.

This attitude is not laziness, nor a lack of ambition on the part of the Peruvian people. It is a combination of unavailable supplies, expense, and only so many hours in a day. The differences of Peru versus the United States go on and on and on. In truth, shouldn't we all start taking more responsibility for avoiding or repairing the holes in our own lives? Life is not predictable, especially once you enter the realms of ritual and magic. Life is surreal. Expect it. Be prepared for it. Use it to your advantage, as would a true Inca.

The zest for life, the celebration of special events, and the love of human nature are the things that make the Peruvian people so special. That, along with their unstoppable, persistent, and adaptable spirit, is truly amazing to see. We all can benefit from emulating these qualities. The most important part of Peruvian magic is the heart energy.

To perform any ceremonies in the correct way, you must begin to love life as the Peruvian people do. They love people. They are wonderfully inclusive, caring, loving, and forgiving. The civilized, modern, and technical part of our world is truly suffering from poverty, chiefly a poverty of spirit. Most Westerners who have homes, health, jobs, family, and friends are so busy working, worrying, and protecting what they have that they miss out on joyously sharing life with their loved ones. Fear, greed, and an unwillingness to forgive, risk, or reach out bankrupts most Western lives. The Peruvians suffer from little of this. Certainly, they are often poor and sometimes struggle just to survive, but once you get to know them as friends, and not from the perspective of an uncaring, scared tourist, you will find them to be the most generous, sharing, and loving people you have ever met. We need to learn from them, and, ideally, to build our future society based on many of their values. It is their unique energies that have kept Incan ritual and magic alive and evolving. Their unique energies, if emulated properly, will allow you to become a powerful Incan magic worker.

6

Further Incan Rituals

Journal Entry—October 28, 2001: Today we drove to Chinchero, a sweet town about an hour away from Cusco by car. Although a major highway runs through it, Chinchero has managed to retain its pre-Incan ways to a great extent. Its future existence is in question, however, because there is talk of constructing a huge international airport just a few miles away. The plan would be for tourists from all over the world to jet right into the Cusco area, thereby avoiding what some consider the inconvenience of Lima altogether.

But for today, Chinchero remains a simple town. The old Incan Ayllus, or clans, are now represented by a spread-out series of twelve neighborhoods. Each Ayllu has its own rituals and ceremonial leaders. At the beginning of spring each year, just prior to the time to plow the Earth and plant the crops, there is a ceremony for the Virgin Mother. In Peru most of the paintings and even the statues of Mary, the mother of Jesus, are usually triangular in shape. Her head floats on top of a body encased in a broad cape starting thin at her neck and widening to the ground. This makes her appear mountain-like. This was also the shape in which the Incas depicted their Apus, or Mountain Gods. The overlapping similarities between the Virgin Mother and Pacha Mama are also unmistakable. Mary is generally portrayed with the moon below her and the sun above her. This was encouraged by the Catholic clergy to make it easier to switch the people's worship from the Apus and Pacha Mama to the Church. As a result, the worship of Pacha Mama and the Apus continues, subtly, within the confines of Catholic orthodoxy.

As the planting ceremony for the Virgin Mother continues into the night, the separation between Catholicism and the

Incan religious tradition falls away. Each Ayllu group dresses in their distinctive and traditional ceremonial garb. They dance into the church separately, performing a Quechuen ritual that asks the Virgin Mother, the Apus, and Pacha Mama to bless their neighborhoods and the fertility of their fields.

After this ritual, the members of the Ayllu dance backwards out of the church in deepest reverence. Then the next Ayllu dances in for their ritual. This goes on throughout the morning, without the presence of a priest or church official. This powerful ritual is undoubtedly similar to those first performed as much as 2000 years ago. Chinchero has survived in relative prosperity, with bountiful harvests as the norm, right up to the present day. Will this or any ritual protect the village and its Ayllus from an international airport? Only time will tell.

Chinchero

In Chinchero, they grow delicious potatoes. We arrived at the right time of year, and were treated to Watia, which is something like a celebratory Quechuen barbecue. Of course, it's probably very different from any barbecue you've ever seen. They first gathered many dirt clods from the field and arranged them in a hive or an adobe style oven, one with a small opening in front. Then they began a fire with eucalyptus branches. When the dirt clods were very hot, a great many potatoes were dumped into the opening onto the hot coals. Then the dirt clod oven was caved in with short logs and hoes. The caved-in clods were covered with dirt and the whole pile left baking for an hour. When we returned, they dug up the dirt and clods with sticks and hoes and pulled out the perfectly cooked potatoes. These were gathered into a blanket and carried to a central place where everyone could join in on the feasting. We were served locally made hot sauce and cheese with the hot potatoes. We sat with a group of people who lived in Chinchero and who had been doing traditional weaving all morning. We ate and laughed while peeling the potatoes by hand and consuming them smothered in sauce.

Yes, Chinchero is a typical Peruvian village, torn between the Western world (blue plastic tarps and plastic rain ponchos are very evident) and the traditions of the Incan and pre-Incan cultures.

Assuming the Energy of the Gods and Goddesses

As I have stated, I believe that the Incan Gods and Goddesses do exist and have had an affect on human life for centuries. The Incan deities function as archetypes in my mind, heart, and spirit. To me, an archetype is a being that is larger than life; they do not necessarily have to be immortal. Poets struggle, rebel, and touch the divine with their creativity. Artists starve and are misunderstood, but they inspire many with their works. Teachers are underpaid and overworked, but they are the co-creators of our future and the molders of youth. Mothers are often overwhelmed, but they are also nurturing and able to accomplish an amazing array of tasks with great skill. Successful business people can be heartless and driven or they can be creative and highly intuitive. Publishers are eccentric guides of the sacred trust. They co-create and disseminate important information for all people. It is a challenge for mindful people to hold the same or similar jobs for any period of time and not to take on our society's archetypal images of that job. Those who succeed excel in their chosen field. Gods and Goddesses have similar challenges. You can often figure out what work a person does by how they dress and how they behave.

The Incan Pantheon

The Incan pantheon was once worshipped by a powerful Empire. Many members of that pantheon have been forgotten, while others were ignored for centuries. Gods and Goddesses love attention, just like children and animals. They have immeasurable amounts of energy, power, insight, and ability that they are more than willing to share with you. The first step is to select the deity that best represents who you are and who you want to be.

By picking one deity whose aspects you admire and wish to emulate, you can begin a spiritual practice of enhancing your life and way of living. You must remember that these are truly radiant God beings! They can light fire under your life and your ambitions, but remember that this is a serious exercise. Once you begin praying to and/or meditating on one being, there is a certain amount of give and take that can be challenging to control. As with societal archetypes, there are positive and negative energies attached to each deity. You must remain vigilant to take in and build on the positive aspects and repel the negative energies. Being mindful of this is the most effective tool to achieving it. If you feel that you are becoming ungrounded, are easily tired, or suffer any ill effects of any kind, simply pray to the deity you are invoking and specifically ask them to enhance rather than lessen your energies. If you feel or observe negative affects creeping into your life, just thank them for their offerings and request that they go elsewhere and leave you alone. That's all it takes. Even though you are interacting with Gods, your requests must be honored. There are many Incan deities from which you might choose. Wiracocha, Vira, or Inkariy, each a representation of the Incan Creator God, is a glowing and artistic entity. His imagination and persistence were essential in helping give birth and direct the essences of the Peruvian cultures, culminating in the Incan Empire. His energies can greatly increase your creative abilities, inspiration, and wisdom.

Inti, the Sun God, is a fiery figure. Meditating on Inti is easiest while feeling the rays of the sun on your face. His energies bring light and growth into your life. Inti's energies can increase your ability to be warm, loving, and compassionate. They can also help you attract powerful positions and execute your responsibilities wisely.

Pacha Mama is Mother Earth Goddess. Today, she is also contained in and contains the essences of the Christian Mother Mary. All aspects of nature, birth, and the mothering instinct are important parts of Pacha Mama. Her energies are of nurturing, of love, of growth and fertility. Pacha Mama's energies are in many ways the energies of the twenty-first century. This is a time when the feminine energies are rising and gaining strength, shepherding all of humanity towards a more harmonious role with nature. Pacha Mama's energies are helpful for better parenting, for farming, or for growing a business. Her energies provide a kind of knowledge that is nonverbal, ancient, and powerful yet vulnerable at the same time.

Pacsa Mama or Mama Quilla is the beautiful, silvery Moon Goddess. The moon is a figure of mystery and romance. Her energies can bring you elegance, understanding, and insight into areas and things that are difficult to understand. Her energies can help cure mental problems and worries. The moon energies also increase psychic abilities. The invocation to Pacsa Mama follows this list.

Mama Occala is the Goddess of the Oceans and Waters. She is represented as a woman with scales and hair of seaweed. Her energies are very soothing. They assist with adapting to change and reducing stress.

Liviac the Lighting God is a living lighting bolt. His essence is electricity, and his energies can reinvigorate people lacking in physical energy. Liviac can also assist in dealing with shock or loss. His energies light up unseen possibilities.

Chuqui Yllayllapa is the Thunder God. He appears as a fierce royal Incan warrior until he just explodes in a huge thunderclap. His energies bring surprise and assist in coping with loud or bothersome noises. He also provides insights into elements that may have unseen effects on your life. His energies can assist you in becoming more visible, respected, and noticed, perhaps even famous.

Kuntur, the Condor Goddess, is an Incan woman with large brown wings and, quite often, a beak instead of a nose and mouth. She can transform into a condor and fly to the highest heights. Her energies are extremely positive, providing different perspective into a situation or organization. The condor energies will assist in ridding you of aspects or things in your life that are dead or that no longer serve you, as well as experiencing the freedom and magic of spiritual flight.

Q'enti, the Hummingbird God, is similar to Mercury, the messenger God of Roman mythology. His energies allow you to reach your goals faster, and they are also excellent for teaching and disseminating information. When you have a day with too much to do, invoking Q'enti will assist you in achieving more and feeling fulfilled.

Guanocvicuna, the Llama God, had the head, neck, and hind feet of a llama and the hands and body of a human. His energies increase endurance and help practitioners succeed against great challenges. These energies help you to make decisions about how much you can achieve, and they also help to ensure independence. Invoking Guanocvicuna helps to maintain a wild will and spirit while still living a domesticated or civilized existence, allowing you to expand your abilities to assist others in living better lives.

Puma Orqo, the Puma Goddess, has the head and face of a puma, with pawlike hands. Her energies can assist you in becoming fierce and fast, a great tracker, and a wonderful parent.

Chaven, the Warrior God, is an unstoppable warrior made of stone. He holds a rod in each hand and has an amazing set of teeth. His energies give strength, for all life is a challenge to the true warrior. These energies allow you to achieve almost anything. They allow you to maintain your dedication and discipline in the face of long odds, but they also allow you to know when a wise retreat will allow you to fight and win another day.

The Weeping Goddess is Chavene, the sister of Chaven. She looks similar to Chaven but cries bloody tears, symbolic of her position as the Goddess of Emotions. She can assist you to allow yourself time and space to grieve loss, to be depressed, to be vulnerable, and to be sensitive and sympathetic. Chavene's energies are about being stronger by being able to be weak. The oak tree is blown down in a strong wind, but the willow bends. Chavene is as strong as an oak, yet able to bend and cry like the weeping willow.

Mama Hanka is the Fertility Goddess. She often appears as a human corncob of bluish hue, with hair of corn silk. Her energies assist with adaptability and resilience, as well as multiplying one's resources. One kernel of corn, planted and tended properly, can bring forth a harvest of many ears with many kernels on each. So it is with Mama Hanka's energies.

One of my favorites is Kuru, the Corn Worm God. His energies are those of an insect who has become a God against all odds. His main characteristics are persistence, practice, and patience. He is like the ant that moved the mountain; the odds are not important. It takes many swings of a hatchet to chop down a cedar tree, but repeated blows will achieve any goal. Kuru energies are for achieving the nearly impossible.

The Incan pantheon was extensive. Most of the Gods and Goddesses had the ability to alter their form from pure light to their natural appearance, whether it be an animal, a rock, or a bird. They could also assume human form at their will. It is not difficult to make up your own ritual to take on the personality, knowledge, and skills of each God and Goddess.

Invoking Pacsa Mama and the Energies of the Moon Goddess

One of my favorite Goddesses is Pacsa Mama. She is the Moon Goddess, beautiful, silver, sensual, mysterious, and pregnant with possibilities of the unknown. I love her because, as the moon, she is the figure of transformation and romance.

Here is a wonderful beginning to your meditation on Pacsa Mama. First get comfortable, and then allow yourself to reach a deep sense of relaxation. Imagine a column of energy going forth from your toes, all the way up your body, and out your forehead and the top of your head; this energy will reach out to the moon.

Here it collects a column of moonlight that contains all the inspiration and nighttime energies that you will share with the moon. Draw this column of light back to Earth and into you. You'll feel yourself physically filling up with it in your forehead region, and spiritually through your sense of intuition. Allow the energy to flow into your throat and down your arms to your fingertips, where it will light up your creative abilities. The moon has inspired creation throughout history; so it will be with you.

Next, bring the column of moonlight into your chest area, focusing on the heart. The moon has inspired romance and love more than most other elements in this realm. Let it ignite these passions within you. Move the energy into your stomach and the other organs. The moon often lets people know when they are not centered. It brings out fears and feelings of loneliness, sickness, weakness, or depression. Yet, if you can transform these energies and find your radiant health, joy, balance, and strength by moonlight, you can be comfortable and function well under any circumstance.

Now bring the moon energies to your sexual organ; this is the seat of passion and lusts, not just for sex but also for all aspects of life. If you lust for any goal and bring passion to whatever you do, then nothing is impossible for you. The moon energy of Pasa Mama can always help you do these things. Her energies also enhance sex and love. Let the moonlight pour down into you, filling the base of your backbone and flowing down your legs to your feet and the tips of your toes. These are your areas of survival and foundation. Fill them with Pacsa Mama's moonlight energies. As you do, feel your life improving everywhere. Enhance the best of what your childhood years gave you and feel the worst memories and experiences fading like the sunset. Feel the realignment of your life energies. The moon will firm and strengthen the very foundation of your being. The Incan messenger runners, who were fastest by moonlight, were the most respected and rewarded because they were the ones that could run fast under any circumstances. Your feet are swift, strong, and steady. Your foundation is strong as an Incan rock structure bathed in moonlight.

Now feel the presence of Pacsa Mama. Feel her love and radiance and moonlight overflow and pour out from every molecule and cell of your body. Then say aloud, "Thank you, Pacsa Mama. I want to share your existence. I want to embody the essence of you—the intelligent, adaptable, and mysterious moon." Each day for a full moon cycle (28 days), spend time staring at the moon and repeating this exercise. Read more about Pacsa Mama and moon deities of other cultures. Find out all you can about the moon itself. Write about it; meditate on all aspects of being the moon. When you feel you have become as much of the moon and Pacsa Mama as you can be, give thanks. Then take a few days off before you choose your next Incan deity. For this meditation can and should be adapted for evoking the essences, attributes, and energies of any deity.

Death and the Dead as Allies

In most Peruvian rural villages, the old ways manage to live on. One of these old ways, in addition to the prayers to nature deities, is ancestor worship. Ancestor worship is dealt with at length in the literature about the Incas. It was an important part of their culture, as it was with many Asian cultures. An aspect of it in Peru today is called *Gentil Mach* ancestor, worship, which is connected to caves or ruins and can provide guidance or curses. *Huk Kaq Vida* is the other world, the other life where those that have died go. The way the former Sapa Incas' mummies were treated as living Gods is an indication of the high regard in which the dead were held. In Incan and pre-Incan times, it was customary to mummify your revered ancestors and keep their bodies for future consultation. The Incas knew that the veil between the realms of the living and the dead was not thick and that it could be easily penetrated. Most villages believed that there was a cave or lake or forest grove near their village where the spirits of the dead often congregated, either with the intent of reincarnating as a newborn infant or just to visit the familiar energies of their most recent life. Most villages had someone who would perform rituals to contact a dead relative or former village elder for comfort or advice. The rituals varied from village to village and from region to region, however, the basic elements and forms were the same.

In life many if not most people fear death. I was personally blessed in this life to have had a father and grandfather who were morticians and funeral directors. Actually, I was in line to inherit the family funeral home and take over the family business. I apprenticed to my father for years and attended the embalming college at Gupton's Embalming and Funeral Directing School on the Vanderbilt campus in Nashville, Tennessee. It was in Nashville that I decided that assisting families with the loss of a family member was noble work. It also paid very well. However, in planning to work so intimately with death, I first had to overcome my fear and look at death as an ally, not an enemy. This caused me to changed my mind, and decided to dedicate my life to exploring and sharing open-minded and open-hearted spirituality. But my years in that profession allowed me to learn to become familiar with death as one of my most powerful allies! The Incas had many rituals for contacting the dead. I began to add some into this book and thought better of it, because fear is like a cancer! Most people live in fear of death. That lessens the fullness and quality of their life. My strong advice to all readers is to first become a fearless Incan warrior. Then if you choose to, it will be a simple matter to speak with the dead.

Offering of the Essence

One of the living practices of the Andean people, which is very basic yet quite important, is called the offering of the essence. It consists of offering small portions of foods and liquids that are to be consumed by sprinkling or blowing them toward the deities. *Samincha*, means "sharing food or drink with the deities." The fragrance of the burning coca leaves is blown toward a given mountain Apu or Pacha Mama. In the case of a drink or *ch'allay*, some is poured or sprinkled while reciting, "To you, Apu, we give this offering."

Pachatierra is the earth shade, the evil sister or malevolent aspect of Pacha Mama. We all have a dark side, after all! Unlike Pacha Mama, Pachatierra is a localized deity, which explains why some people get sick when spending time in certain areas. This entity can be placated with offerings of the essence of chicha, food, or coca leaves.

Home Blessing

Partially because of fear of wandering spirits and angry ancestors, and partially because of the benefits of attracting the blessings of Gods and Goddesses and

other spiritual entities, the Incan rituals and ceremonies for building a home are important and should
be adapted to every reader's household. The purpose
of this ritual is to maintain the stability and safety of
the dwelling. It is for this purpose that before the
ground is opened for the foundation, payment is made
to the Earth (*Pago a la Tierra*). The people of the Andes
are aware that the Earth is a living entity. Therefore,
they know that the virgin subsoil they are about to
remove is alive. Before digging the subsoil, chicha must
be sprayed from the mouth over the area, while
requesting permission to build from Pacha Mama and
the regional Apus that guard the area.

Once the foundation is dug, the local curandero
places four despachos (offerings) in the four corners of
the house. The offerings are made in harmony, each to a
different element, with uncooked foods. Only the Apus
appreciate cooked despachos. While doing this, a prayer
is said, as follows: "Santa Tierra, sumaqllacta winanki,
winaypaq, winayninpaq." Translated, this means, "Holy
Earth, you will grow well now and for ever." The intention of the prayer is that the house will last forever and
the family will stay united through time.

The four despachos protect and bless the corners of
the house. They keep sickness and misfortune away and
strengthen health and good luck. The ceremony ends
usually by invoking Wiracocha, the Creator God, with
these words; "Sumaqllata llut'ayusyki perqaykita,
allinhatatinaykipaq," which means, "Gently will I plaster
your walls so that you may stand up well." The construction of the house should be viewed as if it was a person with a life of its own. The truth is that every house
symbolizes Pacha Mama.

During the roofing, it is good to purposely make
many off-color jokes and tell sexual stories. This is so

the house might be filled with productive and fertile energies.

With the roofing, the construction of the house is completed. At that point, the *Wasi hun'ay* ceremony is performed. This is an extended Ayllu event, complete with family, friends, and other members of the clan. Everyone brings food and drink. Traditionally, a Godfather to one of the family's children brings the door, but more often these days, the Godparents provides the beer. The Godfather is the one who places the cross and the bulls on top of the door to protect against witchcraft, sickness, and bad luck.

This concludes the ritual of house building, which to me seems very different from having a contractor build it with no regard to earth, neighbors, or spiritual energies. These rituals can be easily adapted to taking possession of a new house, a previously lived-in house, an apartment, or even a room. It is never too late to thank Pacha Mama and recruit the spirit world to bless where you live. This way, your life is likely to be much more fulfilling and productive.

Requesting Favors from the Gods and Goddesses

So rituals and ceremonies are important to every aspect of Quechuen lives. In Peru, when someone requests a *Pacco* or Andean priest or shaman to officiate over an act of Andean liturgy for them, they are first questioned about their motives. If these are found to be legitimate, only then is a date for the ceremony set. Rituals are best coordinated with Mama Quilla, the moon, and stars. To simply ask for the completion of something, as in receiving money owed you, a ritual near a full moon is best. For beginnings, such as blessing a newborn child or moving into a new house, the new moon is superior. The dissipating of energies, as in breaking all ties with a bad relationship or ending a bad streak of luck, is done best in the dark phase of the moon. All these ceremonies are better performed outdoors close to Pacha Mama and the Apus; however, because of health or weather, they may be performed in the home of those requesting the ritual.

A true priest, shaman, or anyone wanting serious results from a ritual will fast for 24 hours prior to the ceremony. This realigns the human physically, mentally, and spiritually. Another way to say it is that fasting sets up a magnetic current in your body and mind that raises their spiritual vibration. While fasting, pure spring water, fresh fruit juice, or coca leaves are the only approved higher vibratory intake.

When all those concerned with the ritual are present, they should be assigned power spots. A truly holy person has an intuitive feel for how individuals' auras and energies subtly interact in a complementary fashion with each other and the Earth herself. Those new to doing this should follow their hunches. Accordingly, the person in charge should instruct people where to stand or sit. This done, the Pacco cleanses the ritual space. This is accomplished both physically and spiritually with prayer. Then the *K'intus*, sacred objects, are properly placed on the chosen altar space. As with those in attendance, the sacred objects are aligned both in an intuitive and ritualistic sense.

Only then does the Pacco begin the ceremony, or *Ninawillca*. This he does whenever possible by starting a small sacred fire. In homes, sometimes a candle must be lit instead for safety considerations. He then fills three separate vessels with wine, chicha, and water. Those asking requests now present him with three coca leaves, which they have carried with them for 24 hours while considering their requests. The Pacco places one of these in the fire, one on the altar, and dunks the third into each liquid. This is returned to the supplicant, who is to chew and swallow it. Now everyone is asked to be fully attentive and then to repeat certain prayers after the Pacco. These might be spoken in Quechuen, Spanish, Latin, or English. The Brazilian version of this ceremony uses Portuguese; the Haitian, Creole; both vary in numerous other aspects as well. The Pacco then address the local, regional, and community Apus. He requests greater humility, insights, and wisdom, and further asks that the petitions be granted. With each request to a different Apu, a flower is floated in the chicha vessel. The Pacco then sprinkles water in the directions of the *suyos*, the four major directions, asking for their blessings and help as well.

He then refeeds the fire. He is often burning cedar, eucalyptus, or anise. He might also burn the dung of a cow, llama, or other animal; at any rate, by this time he has built an impressive little fire. The Pacco continues his prayers, giving thanks that the requested results will be granted, and blessing the altar and all in attendance, first with chicha, then with wine, and finally with water.

The Pacco then burns an offering, which can be money, the request written on a piece of paper, or anything of sacred quality. He begins to clean the altar, burning, as he does, the last coca leaves along with those that he has himself brought. When this has burned completely, he extinguishes the fire. This is often done by covering it with freshly picked wild plants, which have been dampened. Now he bows and kisses the Earth. He then scoops up the ashes and carries them to the highest point nearby, followed by the attendees. He scatters the ashes in the four directions and begs for blessings and assistance of many forces. He then kisses the Earth once more and declares the ritual a success.

A trained Pacco can perform rituals in special ways and to a depth difficult for a novice or amateur to achieve. However, as I have stated, intent, enthusiasm, and desire can bring tremendous results.

Recently, Maria, a friend of ours from Peru had a wonderful woman named Rita visit her. Rita had just received her medical degree at the age of fifty. Rita wanted to perform a ceremony to give thanks and ask blessings on her new career. Maria and Rita went to the Cusco market and purchased a Pacha Mama ritual kit. Then they got themselves to Machu Picchu, where they hiked to the Temple of the Moon. This is a difficult hike that many people do not even attempt. The weather had been rainy for days. They arrived at the Temple and found no one there, which was perfect to perform their ceremony. Maria and Rita apologized for humanities' sins against Pacha Mama and their own negligence to do more in harmony with her. Then they made their requests in the ritual.

As they finished up, the weather cleared. They gave thanks and began the hike back. On the way they heard rustling in the bushes. They checked, and it was an extremely rare Andean bear. They watched it, took pictures, and generally felt blessed. The bear is a symbol of Earth and the warrior and of fierce battles won. When the bear wandered off they got going to catch the bus down. The next day the weather was great, and Rita and her husband Ron went exploring in Machu Picchu. They were near the trailhead to the Temple of the Moon when they again heard a rustling in the brush. It was the bear again. A tour guide came over in awe. "I have been a guide here for ten years and I have never before seen an Andean bear!"

Now all rituals don't receive that level of recognition from Pacha Mama. However, this seems to me a relevant example of how, if done well and in earnest, a modern day Incan ritual will get results!

7

Pisac

*Journal Entry—November 3, 2001: My family and I are on
a bus back to Cusco from the city of Pisac, in the Sacred Valley
approximately halfway between Cusco and Machu Picchu. We
had an amazing adventure in the beautiful and ancient Pisac,
which maintains a strong connection to the ancient ways of the
Incas. This land has its own unique roots, which have largely
resisted the influence of Western culture. What has grown here
is a deeply Incan community that remains very much attached
to the legends, spirits, rituals, and ceremonies of the past.*

*We have now been in Peru for more than two months. Where
has the time gone? Each and every day, Henry and Sophia are
becoming more closely bound to their Peruvian identities. They
are proud to be Peruvian, but I must confess, in their thoughts,
dress, words, and actions, they still come across as Norte
Americano gringos. No matter. They are my beloved children,
and having the opportunity to see them mingle and mesh with
the people and the culture of their homeland is an astonishingly
moving gift for Deborah and myself.*

*The bus is fun, filled with the true sights and sounds of Peru.
Most of our fellow passengers are Quechuen rural folk, carrying
their chickens, potatoes, eggs, and other foodstuffs. The trip
costs two solaces, which comes out to around sixty-six cents in
American currency. The Sacred Valley is appropriately named,
for it passes through some of the holiest places in the culture,
and the crown jewel sits at its far northern end—the world
renowned Machu Picchu. Picturesque Incan terraces and rural
villages dot the landscape rolling by our windows. The weather
is beautiful and clear, and you can see practically forever.*

*We leave for home in a scant seven weeks. I miss my maga-
zines, my work, and the staff at* **Magical Blend.** *Deborah*

misses her work and the ranch. The children miss their friends and even school, a little. There will be good things about getting back to California, but then we will miss dearly what we have here and now. On a day such as this, with the Sacred Valley of the Andes spread out before us, I know that my family believes strongly that there is no place in the world better than Peru.

Ruins

Visiting Pisac was one of the highlights of our Peruvian tour. There seems to be an important connection between the power of ritual and our experiences in Pisac. At any rate, our trip to Pisac was an incredible journey.

Several friends had recommended that we visit the ruins and marketplace of Pisac. I could revisit my favorite ruins 20 times and still get excited and find something new to see. But of course, different is good, too. None of us had ever seen Pisac, which is about a one-hour bus ride from Cusco.

One Saturday, we all woke up early and packed our overnight bags. We walked across Cusco to the bus station and waited for the bus to Pisac. We didn't have to wait long, however, because one leaves every 15 minutes. We were the only gringos on the bus.

There were several small children who were taking the trip to Pisac with us that day. By and large, young kids in Peru were fascinated with Henry and Sophia because they act and talk like they are from a Hollywood movie but their hair and features are obviously Peruvian. They are living many Peruvian children's dreams.

I attempted to speak with some of our fellow passengers during the ride, but had a difficult time properly expressing myself. Henry and Sophia constantly make fun of my Spanish. It's rough, to say the least, verbs in the wrong tense, nouns mispronounced, practically no adjectives or fancy dressings. It is rather ironic that my children's pronunciation and grammar are faultless yet they were shy to speak, while I am not shy to speak in any language, even if I don't know it. However, even with my poor speech, I was able to understand people speaking Spanish as well as the children and Deborah. I'm not sure why, perhaps it's telepathy.

When the bus arrived at Pisac, we were left off with everyone else on the edge of town. We hiked to the Plaza de Armas. Every Spanish-built or Spanish-occupied town in Peru had a Plaza de Armas at the center. Here we had reserved a second floor corner room overlooking the plaza so we could see the small Saturday market break down and the huge Sunday market set up. Our room wasn't ready for us yet, so we left our bags at the hotel for safekeeping and caught a taxi to the top of the ruins. Reaching the ruins by foot requires an exhausting, three-hour hike straight up. The taxi, on the other hand, cost seven American dollars and gets you close to the top in 20 minutes. Not a big decision to be made there.

As soon as we started hiking up from the taxi drop-off point, it began hailing and raining and we got very confused about the trail. That is when Luther appeared, like an angel in the mist. He was actually a 23-year-old metal artist who makes extra cash as a ruins guide. He offered to show us the best parts and explain everything in Spanish for two hours for eight dollars. Why not? Luther was great, filling us in on details about Pisac that we never would have known otherwise.

The Incan city of Pisac was spread out over the top of a long mountain. The Incas had used terracing and build-ings to sculpt the mountain into the form, if seen from the right angle, of a condor. This was the area that served as the Incan graveyard for the region, because the condor was believed to be the bird that escorted the souls of the dead to a better afterlife. The graves, many thousands of them, have all been robbed through the years. A mummy can be sold on the black market for anywhere from $5 to $20,000. With the widespread poverty found in Pisac, this level of plunder, while unfortunate, is not surprising.

The Incas once had crops growing all over both the terraced mountain and in the nearby Urubamba River valley. There was no town on the river until the Spanish took over. Therefore, the Incas climbed up and down the mountain most days! Amazing.

The ruins of Pisac were fantastic, better in some ways than Machu Picchu, in large part because of the absence of *turistocos* (tourists). The rain and hail stopped after a while and that made the experience much better. According to Luther, the Incas had built this city over 1,000 years ago. Many of the buildings were still intact except for their long-gone thatched roofs. We hiked through tunnels, down steep stairs, and onto rock-lined trails hanging off very steep cliffs. We spent extra time at the temples of the sun and the moon. I felt very strong energies at these spots. Centuries of worship build up very powerful energies. I also think that many Incan spirits still haunt these ruins, not wanting to leave their homes. And, of course, there are the nature spirits, the mountain spirits, and the Apus. The Incas prayed to them all fervently, and thus they have more consciousness and awareness than nature spirits in other locales.

We had brought some homemade *empanadas*, Pisac's unique, slightly spicy cheese pockets. We had these and water for lunch with Luther in a watchtower with a breathtaking view of modern-day Pisac, although by most Western standards the city is hardly modern.

The hike down was hot; the sun had come out. We shed our raincoats and sweaters, but still sweated profusely. It took us about an hour to travel back downhill. At Pisac, we bid farewell and thanks to Luther. Back near the Plaza de Armas, our rooms were ready. We washed up and then went back out, exploring the town and the small market. Every aspect of the town was just archetypical Peruvian, and all the people were friendly and sweet. After exploring a while we went back to our room and had Pisco sours, Peru's unique liquor in a tasty mixed drink, which is like a margarita but much better. The kids had Inka cola.

A Night on the Town

Then the surreal, Fellini movie-like energy that suffuses all of Peru really kicked in. The next day, Sunday, was to be Saint Mary's day, but the festivities began that Saturday, with the local band marching around town playing loud, rousing music. Almost immediately after that, Pisac's high school soccer team returned victorious from an away game. They came into town in a dump truck, of all things, screaming like banshees and almost crashing into the band!

The church bells began to ring. This church looked as if it was bombed into silence during the civil war that ended just seven years ago. There are still Shining Path rebels hiding in the Amazon Jungle, but they don't seem to make much trouble and no one bothers with them. We thought that the church was no longer in use, but when the bells rang the lights were turned on and we all went to see the inside. Wow! Ancient, centuries-old paintings and statues surrounded and mixed in with recent Quechuen, modern Incan paintings. Very Incan! Very pagan! Corn and potatoes and Christ dressed in local clothes, worshipping at a sun temple with Apus and condors. Imagine! A church just 45 minutes from Cusco that is very nearly a modern-day Incan temple, with Christ as Inti, the Sun God, and Mother Mary as Pacha Mama.

Four nuns, a priest, and about ten ancient Quechuen grandmothers and their grandchildren came into the church at that point. We left because mass was about to start and we had decided to attend the next morning. Instead, the four of us went back to our hotel's balcony, just in time to watch a new band with native dancers, who, the hotel owner told us, were just for the town, not for tourists. There were only perhaps three other tourists at our hotel, and just a few more in the only other two hotels in town, so it was clear this performance was not for tourists. This was an authentic local celebration.

We went down to the Plaza de Armas and, along with about a hundred locals, witnessed over an hour of bizarre and wonderful dancing. Next came the chicha. Part of the Saint Mary's ritual is that every Ayllu has to supply free dance entertainment and free chicha to everyone in attendance. Understand that these people are poor, dirt poor. Glasses are a rare luxury, generally available only in restaurants and hotels. Most homes have two or three, and that's it. So here come the men from the Ayllu, with a big gasoline can full of very strong chicha and—surprise, surprise—only two big glasses. Every adult who watched the dances must take a big glass full of chicha and drink it down fast, or you will insult the Ayulla. You spray out your last mouthful onto the ground as an offering to Pacha Mama. I drank mine and Deborah drank hers as we were told, in one big, fast gulp. Just imagine guzzling a large glass with an alien taste and an instant, quite intense buzz. Ten minutes later the dancing ended, and we returned to the hotel.

But Saturday was not yet finished. The hotel had an underground sauna, which we had heard was great. We reserved it for Saturday night, at a cost of just ten dollars for the four of us. How could we not try such a unique experience? We got into our bathing suits, took our towels, and climbed down a ladder into the sauna. It was small and very hot! Four people could sit down touching shoulders. They pulled up the ladder and shut the trap door. I added water to the rocks on top of the wood stove and immediately the heat got intense. We all thought we were going to cook the flesh off our bones. The kids almost panicked. It was very strange to be roasting beneath ground, with a lantern and no ladder. I stopped adding water, which made things just a bit more bearable. Deborah was still feeling the chicha, so she got out after about 15 minutes. She knocked on the trap door. The hotel employees opened it and lowered the ladder and she climbed out. The kids lasted another five minutes. I held out for five or ten minutes more. We followed the sauna with cold showers in the room, and then ordered adobe oven baked pizzas, with beer and sodas. After our spectacular, event-filled day, they were the best ever. We inhaled them and went to bed. However, the bands paraded around and preparations for Sunday's huge market went on for most of the night. It was quiet only from about 2:30 to 4:30 A.M. Then the next day began.

The Morning After

I got up at 5:00, and Deborah awoke at 5:30. Together, we went to the 6 A.M. mass. Quechuen mass is simply not to be missed. Hymns being sung in Quechuen are truly heavenly. There is a quality to Quechuen singing that is angelic.

When we emerged from mass, the whole town had transformed into a market, with literally hundreds of booths selling herbs, fruits, vegetables, and crafts. Tourist buses poured into town; we hadn't seen this many tourists in one place in all our time in Peru. Where were they all hiding before that day?

We shopped, explored, watched more bands and different dances. After the night before, we had to pass on more chicha. Instead, we caught the afternoon bus back to Cusco. Arriving back at our home base, we heard news of the latest American attacks on Afghanistan. We all said a prayer for the innocents who would suffer and die. We can all attempt to question what we are told and pray, knowing as we do that in places like Pisac, the energies of life are as wonderful as they could ever be.

8

Incan Dreaming

Journal Entry—November 9, 2001: *Tonight, Pacha Mama came back to visit me. It was a dream yet I was not asleep. Or, perhaps, I was asleep yet it was not a dream.*

I was walking in a cool, breezy Andean mountain meadow. Everything was a vibrant, living green. There was a herd of alpacas off to my left and condors above my head, but there were no people anywhere in sight.

Suddenly the ground in front of me shook and began to rise up, forming a shape that soon resolved into the image of Pacha Mama. She was radiant and beautiful, looking young and ancient all at once. Her clothes were made up of leaves and rocks and feathers, an amazing amalgamation of matter from all elements of nature.

Pacha Mama smiled at me and spoke. "Michael Peter, it is wonderful to stand face to face with you again. I wanted to reassure you that you are on the right path at last. Bringing your family to Peru, living in Cusco, and sharing with others the spirit and magic of the Incan culture are all worthy efforts. Your connection to the land of the Incas through your children is essential, you must never forget it. This is some of what we had hoped to see from you all these many years. We will continue to support and guide you and your family in your work."

Before I could respond, the dream ended in a burst of wind, a rush of water, an explosion of light. I found myself back in the world that we call reality, happy to have pleased Pacha Mama and the rest of the Incan pantheon.

Now, as I reflect upon my dream and write down these words, I wonder about the nature of dreams, the doorways to dimensions that we can't access any other way. The ancient Incas knew the importance of dreams, and they knew how to interpret their nightly excursions into the astral plane. More importantly, they understood how to use the symbols and signs offered by their dreams in their real lives. We Westerners, with all our Freudian grasping at the essence of ourselves, would be well served to examine this Incan example of dream work.

> In the small rivers of the Amazon jungle there is a small fish. If you catch it, cook it, and eat it in the evening, it will give you great, intense dreams!
>
> —Victor Gurries, *Amazon Guide*, 2001

An Overview of Incan Dreaming

In describing our trip to Pisac, it dawned on me that Peru is very dreamlike. If you have been to Peru, you know the magic that still exists there. If you have not, think of your most magical memories and multiply them times two and you will have a hint of Peru. Peru is like a world of dreams.

The Incas knew the true power of dreams. Humanity flows through history between material identification and a clear insight that the material world we reside in is but a dream. Or, to paraphrase the old children's tune, "Row, row, row your boat gently down the Amazon. Merrily, merrily, merrily, merrily, life is but a dream."

A stone mason once told a close friend of mine, "You can't go slow while you're going fast!" Think about this. It is difficult to be creative when you are attempting to work at a demanding job, raise a family, and fulfill all our modern world's demands. I write best when I can stop my normal day and make time to be alone and focused. This is true of most artists, dancers, actors, and dreamers.

Dreaming is many different things to each one of us. Dreaming is perhaps best represented by an onion. Our spiritual essence has many layers on which we exist, just as our dreams have many levels on which we visit them. They can be a digest of our day. They can be messages from our subconscious. They can be messages from dead relatives, friends, or other entities. We can astral travel in our dreams. We can experience lucid dreaming, when we are awake in our dreams. We can wake up and remember every detail clearly or we can wake up and remember nothing of our dreams. Most of us wake up and remember only chaotic, half-clear, and jumbled experiences and images.

However, the Incas knew that dreaming was theirs to take charge of and utilize to whatever degree they chose. A basic exercise to begin to control your dreams is to say to yourself, "Tonight in my dream I will stop whatever I am doing and look at my feet." It might not occur the first night, but I have worked with many people in dream training, and if you believe that this is doable, repeat it to yourself and keep at it. Within the first week of repeating this message to yourself you will achieve it. When you wake up with a clear memory of having seen your feet in your dream, you have begun to consciously enter your dreams. The second step is a simple task. Tell yourself, " I will eat an apple in my dream tonight," or "I will hike down our street," or " I will talk with my mother in my dream tonight." Again, repeat this to yourself as many times as you can during each day until you wake up remembering having dreamed of your requested task.

A great way to track the progress of your dreams is to keep a dream journal. Set your alarm clock to awaken you early enough so that you will have a half-hour to write down everything you can remember about last night's dreams. This will give your subconscious the message that you want to remember and take control of your dreams. Most people sleep from five to ten hours a night. That works out to a minimum of 1,825 hours, and a maximum of 3,650 hours each year spent sleeping. That's a lot of time that we can utilize to accelerate our spiritual and mental evolution!

Once you have accomplished something simple and remembered it in your dreams, then you can slowly increase the difficulty of your tasks. As with most everything in Incan magical work, start with the simple and slowly increase the difficulty.

Eventually you can go to Peru in your dreams and learn from modern day Incan shamans or dream back in time and experience, as have I, the true pre-Christian Incan Empire. You can even visit other dimensions or different realities.

Dreaming of a Different Reality

There are many accomplishments that can be achieved in the realm of dreams, in this dimensional planet Earth, where I usually reside. I once knew an Incan shaman who was sexually promiscuous. There were always lots of pretty young tourists who wanted to be his students. Temptations are a spiritual test for all of us. Giving into temptation does not always result in dream fulfillment. One of this shaman's student lovers gave him AIDS. He was surprised but knew that this was an opportunity given to him from the Gods and Goddesses to realign his life and the way he had been living. He became celibate, started exercising, and closely watched his diet, eating mostly raw fruit and vegetables, with the occasional cooked meal of traditional potato stew and coca tea. This seemed to slow the progress of the disease, but it didn't stop or cure it.

He chose dreaming as his path to health. One day, he was walking along a mountain stream. He spoke to the spirit of the stream, asking the spirit to allow him to build a healing dream temple along its dreamy shores. He blurred his eyes and stared at the stream. A small stone seemed to be glowing. He waded into the stream and picked up the stone. Then he walked with blurred eyes along the stream bank until a small clearing slightly above and set back from the shore also seemed to glow and almost seemed to be calling to him. Here he placed his stone, gave thanks to the spirit of the stream for its assistance, and prayed that he might return here in his dreams each night and build a healing temple. That night as he fell asleep, he prayed to the stream spirit and other healing energies for assistance in building his healing dream temple. He told himself that his dreams could and would completely heal him.

In his dream journey, he returned to the spot by the stream and found his glowing pebble. He picked up the pebble and it grew in his hands into a large Incan cut stone. He placed it on the ground and looked around to find a nearby pile of these Incan cut blocks. He began lifting the amazingly light stones, placing them end to end as with building blocks.

He awoke before completing this huge task, but felt that he had made great progress. The next day, while awake, he walked the stream. He found another glowing pebble and placed it in his magic spot next to the other one. That night he found the spot and he picked up the second pebble. It too grew into an Incan stone. He continued this same pattern daily for two weeks. He spoke of this as building a healing bridge from the dream world to the material world and back. He told me that you can magnify your desires and intentions from the waking world into the dreaming. Then your bridge can conduct these magnified energies back to day-to-day existence.

At the end of two weeks, my friend had constructed a healing Incan palace in his dreams. Meanwhile, in the real world, he had built a small pile of stones that glowed when he blurred his eyes. For three months, after he finished the construction of his dream healing temple, he would visit it in his dreams at night. During the day, he would meditate at his healing spot by his pile of stones at every opportunity. One night in his dreams, he met a beautiful watery spirit maiden who told him that he was healed. He just needed to scatter his pebble pile for miles along the stream and his healing work was done. However, she warned him that it had been his abuse of authority and the respect paid to him, as well as lack of regard for love and health, that had caused his problems. She ordered him to learn greater appreciation for life and live better in order to stay healthy. When he revisited a medical doctor they were amazed to find he no longer exhibited sign of AIDS or HIV. The dream bridge had healed him completely, some would say, as if a dream had come true.

Ayahuasca and San Pedro

Another friend of mine, Tom Torenez, left his job in San Francisco because he fell in love with a wonderful Peruvian woman. They got married, had two children, and they now own a restaurant in the Amazon. One of the first times I met Tom, he told me of his most intense Ayahuasca dreaming experience. One of his sons was very sick, and the doctors in San Francisco and Puerto Maldonado didn't know how to help him. Naturally, Tom and his wife were out of their minds with fear, as only loving parents with very sick children can be.

Tom decided to visit with a friend who was a native Ayahuasca priest in an attempt to use the herb to find a cure for his son. Ayahuasca is a hallucinogenic vine used for centuries in Andean rituals. He took the Ayahuasca and went to a dream realm where he met a spirit of the plant. Tom asked it for a cure. The spirit refused, telling Tom he had to cure his son himself. Tom asked how, and the spirit answered that Tom already knew how. In desperation, Tom willed himself to the soul of his sick son, speaking to him softly and begging him to heal. A dark shadow emerged from his son and wrapped itself around Tom, smothering and almost drowning him. Tom remembered an Ayahuasca song he had once learned. He sang the song and imagined a green parrot's feather brushing the shadow away as if it were smoke. He heard a scream as the shadow left. He then hugged, kissed, and sang to his son until the child fell asleep.

Tom reawakened in the jungle where he had taken the Ayahuasca, feeling weak and exhausted. He was disappointed, remembering that the spirit had given him no cure for his son. He got washed and dressed and returned as fast as he could to his family. His wife met him at the door with the news that his son's fever and swelling had gone down and he had regained his appetite. Tom went up to his son's room. The young boy awoke and said, "Dad, that was a strange dream with the smoke and green parrot feather. Thanks for the help. Will you sing to me again?"

Tom burst into tears. He had used Ayahuasca dreaming, or Ayahuasca dreaming had used him, to heal his son. That is one of the clearest examples of the power of dreaming and the ways Ayahuasca has been used as a plant ally to expand the possibilities of reality since even before the existence of the Incas.

I once took San Pedro cactus as part of a ritual. I was not used to this substance and had come to the ritual exhausted. I fell asleep, dreaming that I was in a world where there were intelligent plants that swayed as they walked about and communicated by telepathy. Most of these plants looked something like brightly colored sea anemones. I was quite entertained by them until I looked down and realized I was one also. Then I had the true experience of existing, living, thinking, and viewing reality as an extremely alien being. I don't have the words for such an experience. Let's just say that my perspective has never been quite the same.

I should state emphatically that drugs are not necessary to experience powerful magical dreams. They should only be used with guidance and discretion, as tools to explore the many levels of reality—not as toys to escape reality. Some of us don't recall our dreams, but all humans dream every night that they sleep. Humans have always dreamed, both daydreams and deep night dreams. The Incas have taught those who would listen about their beliefs that the dream worlds exist in an enlarged reality and the waking world is truly the illusion. They stated that they could move consciously in dreams and thus could change the material world in mysterious ways. The Incan huacas taught astral travel and control of the dream state as one of the many spiritual skills that initiates with positive intentions and intense practice could learn. Most pre-Christian shamans, medicine people, curanderos, healers, and wise women obtained their community's respect and knowledge to help those requesting it, by traveling in spirit to the realm of death and returning, physically wounded but spiritually wiser. They evolved into super-human spiritual healers, if one is to believe history and the stories still told today. They could reach into the pool of generally untapped human insights and abilities. Because there existed few guide books or maps, each magic worker seemed to develop different wisdom, powers, or abilities and utilized them in very different fashions.

Physical Applications

Many believe the Inquisitions, witch trials, and conquests of Africa, India, much of Asia, and all of Latin America by Christian European countries and agents were all about silencing the old ways. The mostly Caucasian, European, and Christian conquest and homogenization of the world is viewed by many as a huge conspiracy to crush and hide most of the teaching and techniques that encouraged humans to expand their potential. Is the evolution of Western society dependent on crushing the most powerful tool humans have—our imagination?

In Peru, the Conquistadors burned the Quipus. The Quipus were not just calculating tools, they were an entirely new and different way of writing. They were a unique set of keys to a different way of knowing existence and using it to build on itself and evolve. There are so few remaining that their secret language has not yet been deciphered in total.

For the Incas who had the luxury of studying, experimenting, and practicing, dreaming was a powerful tool. In early writings that survive from a few open-minded priests, we learn of shepherds being able to go to sleep and awake knowing where their lost flock was or what herbs would heal their sick animals. They also wrote of the Virgins of the Sun having a more expanded spiritual role than had been previously thought. These Virgins were taught how to focus their feminine energies. Many were able to focus their sexuality into their dreams. Often, they would bring back from dreams instructions or warnings for the Sapa Inca and the Empire.

Dreaming is a tool that is available to all, but few of us chose to practice, learn to control, or utilize these powers. Why not? The Incan visions I have experienced tell me that this is one of the most easily approached and conquered spiritual tools. It is as difficult or as easy as you make it. It is, as with most things, a case of belief, desire, and expectancy. If you only believe, then you can, in reality, wake up in your dreams, experience lucid dreams, and astral travel. If you want to badly enough and are willing to practice unceasingly, you can actually visualize your dream travels. Then the rest is just a flight in the Andes.

Let's restate the basics. You can get answers to difficult questions or be told how to find lost things. You simply have to tell yourself at least three times a day, three times each time, for example, "I will be given the reason I am so attracted to Incan magic in my dreams tonight, and I will remember it clearly when I awake." If you do this as you awake or as you eat breakfast, at noon or lunch, and with dinner but most importantly as you fall asleep, it will happen. If it does not work the first night, (it doesn't for most), it will with repetition each day. Persistence always brings results, no matter the obstacle.

I once heard a story of a magic worker whose village was along the headwaters of the mighty Amazon River. This was during the Shining Path civil war—about 1989. The cocaine growers and the Shining Path revolutionaries were both moving closer to his village and its hunting, gathering, and growing areas. The villagers were frightened beyond belief. Some of the younger families and single people had already left for the far-off cities. In his dreams the shaman asked for answers about how to protect his village from these powerful dark forces. He awoke after a week of no answers and told his fellow villages to begin building big human figures out of vines and weeds. They were to place them around the limits of their territories with signs in Quechuen, Aymara, and Spanish saying, "This land is sacred to the ancient Gods and Goddesses, and it is essential to the very continued existence of all of Peru. Please respect the warnings that they have instructed us in dreams to give you. If disobeyed, they will curse those who trespass and their families."

Both groups stayed completely out of the area. They respected the warnings, until the CIA and United States military occupied it as a base of operations in 1999. However, I was informed by a former American soldier that the use of the village only lasted a few weeks because the Americans and those working for them kept suffering from weird sicknesses and strange accidents. He even added that they all complained of intense nightmares.

Dreaming With a Goal in Mind

If an Inca wanted to become awake in their dreams, they would repeat their desire as a request, nine times in a day. Then eventually one night they would wake up while dreaming, they would stop what they were doing and say their name out loud. They would remember this upon awaking, which was their first step. After they could do this for three nights, they would tell themselves that they would visit a friend in their dream. Each time an action was achieved for three different nights, they would advance. Eventually, I am told, they no longer went to sleep, they simply entered a different dimension in spirit or astral form and they could go where they wished and learn or see whatever they wanted. With practice we are all capable of achieving this level of dream control.

Although you can astral travel in the dream realms and other dimensions, the main aim is to take your consciousness and your astral body out of your physical body and fly to other places on our Earth. A good Incan technique was to fall asleep visualizing your astral body climbing out of your physical body using a vine or rope. It helps to fast or eat lightly, be as relaxed as possible, and not be too tired. The idea is to put your physical body to sleep and go flying to the Andes or the Himalayas or to your lover's house in your astral body. When you succeed you will experience an expanded spectrum of colors and feelings. In the astral plane, this usually feels great. If for any reason you experience fear, always remember that this is only astral weakness. Stop your fear because fear makes you vulnerable, but love and laughter makes you invulnerable. Nothing else but your fear can harm you on the astral plane. You must remember fear is the only thing that can hurt you in the astral or dream dimensions. While astral traveling, I have read secret books in very secured places in other languages, languages that I didn't know how to read. I awake with partial memories of the secrets and teachings I read. The Vatican's sequestered library is a great place to read of lost and hidden knowledge and truths.

I believe I have experienced countless dream states that are somewhere between lucid dreaming and astral traveling. The Incan Gods and Goddesses seem to remember me periodically, and off I go to experience another world, another dimension, or another time as it relates to Incan experience. My dream journals, which help me track and build on my dream successes, over-flow with Incan dreams. I have decoded some of these, but many others were not meant to be fully understood. Rather they were incomprehensibly sent to raise my spir-itual energies. In many ways dreaming is the final fron-tier. It is a tool that many Incas utilized with great skill and at length, as a way to communicate with the Gods and Goddesses, or to study and experience expanded existence. Yet most of us ignore the growth potential con-tained in the dream realm. To become an Incan warrior you must fight that laziness. You must work and learn even in your dreams.

9

Puno, Bolivia, and Tiwanaku

Journal Entry—November 23, 2001: *One of Henry's wishes has been to visit Puno. Eleven years ago, while becoming a family, we were often told that his facial features indicated, without a doubt, that he was from the Puno area. Growing up, whenever he was asked, Henry would always state with conviction that he was born in Puno, Peru, on the shores of Lake Titicaca. Further, he was sure that somehow, his birth parents had moved to Lima and died, leaving him on his own.*

Puno

I had visited Puno and Lake Titicaca for less than a day 28 years earlier and had some nice memories of the area. We began to plan our visit, reading travel books and various reports at the South American Explorers Club. We decided to see Puno, the Uros floating islands, and the ancient tower ruins nearby. Then I read about the timeless ruins of Tiwanaku, which many believe was actually the cradle for the Incan civilization. We made the decision to go ahead and check out La Paz and the ruins. We booked buses (less expensive then airplanes) and budget hotels, and off we went.

The first day we left at 7 A.M. The bus stopped along the way, at an ancient church in Andahahuaylillas, which is called the Cuscaniane Sistine Chapel. The walls and ceilings are painted in minute detail. This church is rumored to hold a great many golden treasures in its basement vaults. The villagers protect it with armed guards around the clock. These old Spanish churches are quite strange and intriguing to say the least.

Our next stop was San Pedro and the ruins of Raqchi. This is a temple that was built by Pachacuteq's father, the Sapa Inca Wiracocha. The ruins are in sight of an inactive volcano and mostly built from lava rock. There were hundreds of silos for storing potatoes, quinoa, beans, and maize. The temple itself was huge and must have been impressive in its day. It is said to be one of the largest Inca complexes built outside of Cusco before Pachacuteq came to power.

We later stopped in Sisuani, a good way south of Cusco. It is a nice little semitourist town where some Peruvian writers and poets live. It is also the capital of Canchis Province. There we were treated to a wonderful five-star lunch buffet in the town's best hotel. Part of our indulgence in booking this trip is that a five-star lunch is included in the fare. It goes without saying that we were happy with our selection of this bus. Delicious soup and delicate sauces, similar to the Peruvian foods and tastes we had experienced, but lighter on meat and vegetable dishes. This was one of the best meals we had during our entire four-month visit.

We arrived at Puno at 3:30 P.M. Our hotel was not world-class but it sufficed, especially since it offered absolutely fantastic views of Lake Titicaca. We spent the first night wandering the walkways around the Plaza de Armas. There were lots of people that looked as if they could be related to Henry, and he enjoyed that. We were tired after almost nine hours on the bus, so we turned in relatively early.

The next morning we took a tour of the floating Uros reed islands. *National Geographic* and the Discovery Channel simply do not do them justice. The Uros people did not want to be absorbed by the Aymara to the east and south or by the Incas to the west and north, so they moved from the shores of Lake Titicaca and decided the only way to stay independent was to stay unapproachable. They used the reeds that grow in the lake to make islands. They wove the reeds in huge tick mats that floated and were water-resistant. They were so strong that they built villages on them and anchored them far out in the middle of the lake. This kept them safe from both the Aymara and Incas. They remained completely independent until the Spanish arrived. The Spanish couldn't conquer them, but the missionaries moved onto the islands with them and greatly altered their way of life and thinking. The Uros language now is gone, replaced by Spanish, Aymarary, and Quechuen. The amount of rheumatic diseases from living on the islands is extremely high, and it begins in 20-year-olds. Many Uros descendants have moved to villages on the shore of the lake, but the old ways do continue. There are many active villages on the islands. They get much of their food by fishing and hunting on the lake. There are active grammar schools with good teachers on most islands. We got to ride on a reed boat between islands, which was a unique experience. The people were friendly and informative. The islands open to the public do derive most of their income from tourism, but so does much of Peru. These islands show us how very different life can evolve when there is a will for independence and a sense of the importance of defending one's beliefs.

We got back to Puno, had lunch, and then were off to the Sillustan Atuncolla. These ruins are believed to belong to the long-vanished Colla tribe. Little is known about these people, who dominated the Titicaca area before the Incas. Some feel the towers they left were burial crypts for their royalty. The towers are called *Chupas*. The largest stand about 36 feet tall and are generally found on the Umaylo peninsula. Their stone work is more complex than that of the Incas, with exquisite carvings of lizards. The only way to enter these towers is through a tight crawl space. But why, if these were burial towers, were no bodies or death offerings ever found? I strongly feel that the generally accepted dating of this site is far off. Scientists will tell you that this area dates to only 2,000 years ago, but I believe that the Sillusta Atuncolla ruins were and are related to Tiwanaku and are, therefore, truly ancient. The Incan legends say that they were built by the race of giants who lived before human beings; who, in fact, lived before the earth assumed its present distance from the sun.

Leave it to Peru, every day seems to be a holy day and cause for celebration. Our second night in Puno was the night of the Holy Spirit! The businesspeople, army, and prosperous households blocked off the streets, and, in front of the buildings, they created elaborate colored sand and flower-petal paintings, about 15 by 20 feet rectangular, of the Catholic Holy Spirit. Each participating group erected an altar. At about 5:00 P.M. the army band, led by priests and other important religious people, paraded in front of a heavy statue mounted on logs of the Holy Spirit. The statue was carried by army officers who balanced the logs on their shoulders. The parade marched right over these exquisite sand paintings, which took all day to create, destroying them in the process. They then stopped to pray at the altars, while fireworks exploded overhead.

After the prayers at each altar, the band played on and the march continued to the next sand panting.

Everyone but the soldiers were dressed in purple. The festival is all about requesting miracles from the Holy Spirit for the upcoming year. I prayed for this book to have a great effect on many lives and for our children's teenage years to be pleasurable for our family. There seemed to be lots of drinking, but no free, compulsory chicha. That was all for the best as far as I was concerned. After the miracles parade we went shopping in the street booths of Puno and found some great bargains. Henry, in particular, discovered some great Puno memorabilia. He wanted to take home some things from this city of his birth. We went to bed about 9:30, but someone, either a late arrival from the rural areas or some group who wouldn't stop celebrating, marched by the hotel well after midnight, loudly banging a drum, playing flutes, and carrying a smaller statue of the Holy Spirit. The religious celebrations just never seem to stop in Peru.

The next morning the sunrise over Lake Titicaca was fantastic. We had a good Peruvian breakfast, and at 9:00, we caught the bus into Bolivia. We had very little trouble with immigration, with the small exception that Sophia has grown so much that they were not sure it was her passport. Once we established that she was who we said she was, we had no further problems.

Copacabana

Three hours after leaving Puno, we arrived in Copacabana, Bolivia. It is a lovely and quaint resort town on the western shore of Lake Titicaca. We got a luxurious room in an impressive hotel; because it was midweek, we received a very affordable rate. The huge beds allowed us to look through voluminous picture windows overlooking the lake. We went to the main cathedral, the Church of Miracles. For some reason I never learned, it looks very much like a Moslem mosque. The walkway to the church is lined with sick and aging beggars. The cathedral houses the black Madonna of Copacabana, and if you pray to her, she is said to grant miracles. In front of the church you can buy little models of your dream house, dream car, college diploma, stack of dream money, dream grocery store, or just a great general totem of the future. We each bought a miracle and went in to pray, giving coins to the poor beggars who lined the walkway. The inside of the church is well maintained in the classic style. On the way out, they sell miracle water.

We climbed Calvairio, a steep cliff that overlooks the port. It was a religious center when Tiwanaku was at its height. The locals still celebrate amazingly involved ceremonies here; in fact, Copacabana remains a pilgrimage site for spiritual seekers from all over Bolivia. It is the site of a massive spiritual gathering each summer. When the Incas took over this area, in about 1350 C.E., the locals rebelled on a regular basis. They would alter all the ceremonies the Incas demanded for the Temple of the Sun and the Temple of the Moon. Thus, with the arrival of the Spanish a few centuries later, the tradition of subterfuge was well established.

The *Kallawayas*, traditional pre-Incan priests, still perform rituals on Calvairio. Despite a great many crosses and other signs of Christianity, the local Kallawaya will cleanse you spiritually, help cast spells, draw your dreams to you, and read your coca leaves—all for a nominal cost. Yet all of this is done in Spanish with Bolivian Aymara accents. From the top of Calvairio, we saw the glorious sunset over Lake Titicaca.

The night was spent playing ping-pong and shooting pool back at the hotel. I am by far the worst in the family at both, but we all laughed and had a wonderful time. We ate at a great restaurant. The food was slightly different and we paid for it with Bolivian bolas. Different currency and different foods take a little getting used to. The next morning we climbed Intiwatana, a pre-Incan astrological observational temple. There were other ruins surrounding us on all sides, but we hadn't anticipated it and didn't allocate enough time. We later realized that we could have taken boat rides to the islands of the Sun and Moon. These amazing ruins are said to be the birthplace of the Incas. Try as you might, you just can't see everything in one visit.

We enjoyed another nice lunch and caught a bus to La Paz, the City of Peace. It used to be the City of the Potatoes, but they thought that was a bit too rustic, not cosmopolitan enough. At almost 4,000 meters (more than 12,000 feet), it is the highest capital of any nation in the world. I lost my breath from time to time, which is a common occurrence—the lung capacity of those not born at these altitudes just isn't large enough to grab adequate amounts of oxygen. Those whose ancestors have been born for generations at these high altitudes have different lungs, spleens, and even blood, as compared to those of us born at lower altitudes. The dentist in our town of Chico, California had to conduct a fair bit of research on how to use analgesic gas for Henry as a child because his physiology is so different.

La Paz

La Paz is in a big valley. As you enter the city, you look down the edge of the mountains onto a community that looks like an alien Chicago. It has 800,000 people and very few trees, yet lots of high rises and other buildings, all stacked wall to wall. Our hotel was nice and quite affordable, and our room was on the tenth floor with a view of the downtown. The first night in La Paz gave all of us a severe case of culture shock. It is a good deal different from Peru—for instance, the shoeshine boys wear black ski masks to hide their identities from schoolmates. At first, we were unsure what to make of that. La Paz is very different than Lima, Cusco, or Puno. We had New York pizza that first night for supper, because the names of the foods in all the other restaurants were incomprehensible to us, even though they were in a dialect of Spanish. The pizza, beer, and sodas made us feel more in control. We wandered the markets for two hours. They sell everything but they don't haggle over the prices—miles of barbershops, underwear stores, and perfume sellers; booth after booth after booth. It was Saturday night and there was lots of music in the streets. Even after we returned to our hotel, the noises from the street drifted up to our room until the wee morning hours.

The next day we took a tour of the Valley of the Moon. The south side of La Paz is where the rich live, in amazing mansions that are very impressive. Nearby was the valley; it has a rather desert-like atmosphere, and the erosion has formed intricate sculptures in the sand, thus the name the Valley of the Moon. We hiked about and saw the natural sand formations. We also saw the highest golf course in the world and a number of foreign embassies.

Then we went on an extensive tour of the city. I could easily fill a book just writing about Bolivia and La Paz. The area was the least favored of all the land that the Spanish conquered, and it is perhaps the least popular destination in today's South America. Bolivia and La Paz even get talked down in the guidebooks. The nation is third in the Americas in terms of poverty, following only

Haiti and Guyana, yet the people have an indomitable spirit, with a tangible streak of Bolivian pride. My family greatly enjoyed La Paz and all we saw in Bolivia. Henry said he would enjoy living there. Sophia, on the other hand, preferred Copacabana.

At my request, we ended our tour at the witches' market. Blocks of booths selling potions, offerings to the Gods, and ingredients for rituals. I was tempted to buy a llama fetus, used for sacrificial offerings, but I purchased a few potions instead. One is made of certain frog parts, duck eggs, Maca, and other herbs. It is supposed to increase your intelligence and sexual pleasure. We shall see.

On Sunday night we went to a *Pena*, which is a dinner performance of Bolivian folklore. We had asked our guide to explain the menus to us and, therefore, we ate well. It's so much easier to enjoy your meal when you know what you are ordering and eating. I had llama steaks and Deborah had the pork, lamb, and potato stew for which Bolivia is famous. The Pena was at a dinner club called Huri. We were thrilled because it was as amazing a display of dance and music as we have ever experienced. The bands played a mix of traditional instruments and modern brass. The key instruments were the *zamponas* (Panpipes), a wide variety of flutelike wind instruments, and the *charangos*, which are little guitars made from armadillo shells.

The music was so other-worldly that it reminded me of the bar scene in the original *Star Wars* movie. There were traditional Inca, Aymara, Wari, and Spanish dances, all performed with enthusiasm and skill. We got there early and sat right near the stage. However, we didn't realize that in sitting so close, the performers would insist that we join them on stage and dance a couple of dances with them. Henry and Sophia loved it, Deborah was okay, and I danced not so great—of course. We laughed and made the most of it.

That night, we witnessed the intense dances of the Bolivian miners. It has been said that enough gold and silver was taken out of Bolivia to build bridges from La Paz to Barcelona, Spain and back. The lives of the coca-leaf–chewing Bolivian miners have always been torturous and difficult, if not deadly. Their dances reflect the energy that comes from living life on the edge of death. Then there were the Afro-Bolivian music and dances. In an attempt to improve production in the mines, massive amounts of slaves were imported from Africa. The problem is that the mines were and are almost all in extremely cold mountainous areas—places in which the tropical African people fared poorly. In order to protect their investments, the slave owners sold those who survived to plantation owners in the Bolivian part of the Amazon jungle. Their descendants eventually earned their freedom, and there, in the Amazon, they have survived and prospered. Their music and dance were overflowing with the feeling and depth reflected in their struggles and the clash of cultures. This was followed by the Amazonian witch-doctor selections. These were my favorites—the puma hunt, the parrot worship, and the wizard's blessing. All overflowed with implied magic and symbolism.

The evening concluded with a blessing and dance dedicated to Pacha Mama. The show was wide in scope and all four of us laughed, cried, and were deeply moved. I was left with the feeling that Bolivia's people, in spite of all their suffering and setbacks, have a deep sense of pride and spirit that will see them through to a better future. I insisted that we walk back to our hotel at 11 P.M. through the wild La Paz streets. We got back to the hotel just fine on foot. For all its poverty and homelessness, La Paz is actually very safe, with a low crime rate.

Tiwanaku

The next day we tackled Tiwanaku. According to the experts, Tiwanaku is the most difficult pre-Incan society to explain. This ancient settlement exercised a major influence on the entire Andes region from 1500 B.C.E. until 1000 C.E.—just one hundred years before the Incas took over. My contention is that Tiwanaku was tied in to the fabled sunken continents of Atlantis or Lemuria. I further believe that this area was deserted many centuries before the Incas came to power. Whatever your beliefs, I found Tiwanaku to be fantastic—even more impressive than Machu Picchu, if that is possible.

Most of the ruins at Tiwanaku have not been excavated due to lack of funds, trust, and security. The last anthropological dig in the early nineties was caught smuggling out millions of dollars of gold and treasures. There has been no research allowed since. However, the ruins that have been excavated and preserved are simply beyond imagination. In the ruins there are stone carvings of elephants, statues of seahorses, and other kinds of fish found only in the Southern Pacific Ocean. There are statues of people undeniably from China, others from Mongolia, still others from Africa. Some closely resemble the statues of Tibet, and others the heads of Easter Island. There is even an ancient sculptured head there that Erich von Daniken, author of the book, *Chariots of the Gods* believed to be an alien. It looked like a classic gray alien to me. The grays were brought to public notice by Whitley Striber's book, *Communion*, and have been reported by countless abductees. Most of the skulls found at Tiwanaku were higher and narrower than those of normal humans. It is speculated that this was done for aesthetic or religious reasons by binding the heads of young children. Then there are the Incan legends of the

Nawa, the race of giants that reportedly lived in Tiwanaku before the humans. These legends lend credence to the theories of Tiwanaku having been a seashore resort in Lemuria after the lost continent sank. Lemuria was thought to be inhabited by giants, strange skull-shaped humanoids, and humans. The far eastern shore rose to become the Himalayas. Meanwhile, it is estimated that the Andes rose approximately 50,000 years ago, bringing Tiwanaku to its present height.

As recently as 1995, Carol Cumes, in her book, *Journey to Machu Picchu*, explains how she was shown giant skulls and bones of what she calls the Machuckuna. She was told they were an ancient pre-Incan race. A local farmer showed her these artifacts, which he considered to be very sacred. Although they were well hidden in a difficult to reach cave, the farmer made Carol pledge not to reveal their location.

The pyramids at Tiwanaku are all multileveled and astrologically aligned. The water-drainage systems are all at a nearly perfect two-degree pitch and function well after being buried in dirt for centuries. The stone work is more intricate than that of the Incas. The whole megalopolis, aside from one temple and some of the larger statues, was covered in dirt ten to fifty feet deep. Why or how, no one seems to understand or be able to explain. The Incas, the Spanish, and later the local Bolivians dug up and stole, defaced, and destroyed many valuable statues and treasures. The studies of pre-Colombian times confirm that Tiwanaku launched the first and most likely the oldest technical revolution in the world. There are respected scientists that state that it is likely that Tiwanaku is as old if not older than the Sphinx and all the ruins of Egypt! Even the minimal excavations that have been done thus far prove that medicine, cranial operations, and the use of quinine were all practiced in early

Tiwanaku. These all required specialists trained in these areas of medical practice. How did this come about? These Tiwanakan doctors seem, from the evidence, to have extensively researched the medical properties of multitudes of plants whose benefits are still used today.

There was another artifact that I found hugely fascinating and mysterious. On the north wall of Kalasasaya, the Temple of the Stones Standing Up, there are two blocks far apart that work as broadcasting and auditory devices. There are holes cut in the shape of ear channels. When you speak normally into either one you can be heard all over the temple area. When you place your ear up to the opening you can hear conversations a football field's length away. The early inhabitants of these lands must have had an extensive understanding of stone carving and acoustics to accomplish this.

In Tiwanaku, there are numerous works in stone with fine carvings, as if these people wanted their messages to be eternal. The Solar door has a calendar of 52 weeks, four seasons, and 365 days. I found that impressive. Earlier, it was believed that all the Tiwanakan carvings were only for aesthetic purposes, with the function of decorating existing pieces. Recent studies, however, show that most carvings were previously designed and planned before being worked in stone and that they contained messages of astronomical, mathematical, and geometrical nature. Was this a written message to the future and will we ever decode them? I can hardly wait to find out.

Not only did the Tiwanakans develop architecture, genetics, engineering, medicine, herbology, and other sciences with great success, they were also able to develop the arts to a very high level. Their ceramics, knitting, weaving, and craftsmanship in precious metals, stone hewing and carving all hint at an exquisitely creative ability.

Above all, it was a political organization based on solidarity and reciprocity that allowed the Tiwanakans to perform great work and create a profoundly humanistic society. This is reflected in their refined handling of rocks as well as in their exceptional artwork. They seem to have believed strongly that Earth was created for people, and everyone had a responsibility toward Earth and all other humans. This seems to have been a widely held concept in which humans, like the planets and stars, were part of a cosmic equilibrium.

It can be stated that Tiwanaku, in all areas, was clearly an important center of ancient wisdom and science. The Tiwanakans spread their control using the principle of reciprocity, sending out well-trained specialists to share their knowledge with other peoples. They showered these neighboring tribes with gifts that demonstrated their technological advancement. In return, they requested that the new peoples join the loose federation of Tiwanakan trade. In this way they had friendships and intricate, peaceful relationships with even the most fierce Amazon jungle tribes. The influence of the Tiwanaku federation extended from present-day Ecuador in the north to Chile in the south. It covered most of Peru and Bolivia, much of northern and central Argentina, and an indeterminate amount of the Brazilian Amazon. The knowledge of the Andean world came together here long before the Incan Empire even began to take form. It is unclear when or how the Tiwanaku influence ended, or why the main centers were deserted. One questionable theory speculates that neither war nor disease ended Tiwanaku; rather, several generations before the Incas came to power, a drought lasting over 100 years hit much of the extended Tiwanaku federation. The stress from a lack of food and water ended their great accomplishments. But the question of who selectively covered this huge area with deep dirt, as well as how and why, remains to be explained. Despite the numerous unanswered questions, I was terrifically pleased to have visited this cradle of civilization.

Back to Cusco

That night my family and I did last minute shopping and went to bed exhausted from a mind-stretching day. The next day was Tuesday, and we began the 20-hour stretch of bus rides back to Cusco. We started at 8:00 A.M. We had an hour-and-a-half layover in Copacabana for lunch, and then recrossed the Bolivian border. We had a four-hour layover in Puno.

Somewhere in Puno, Henry lost his camera, which I felt was symbolically important. It seemed like the universe's way of helping Henry to grieve for his sense of personal loss in Puno—for another life that would have been very different if he had grown up there, but that was not meant to be. It was also, perhaps, his unconscious way of giving something as an offering to Puno in return for the city's gift of his life. Hopefully, the person who found it had their life made better in some small way. Henry was appropriately sad until he fell asleep on the bus.

The rest of us were nothing but relieved to be on the way back to our temporary home. Although it was a fantastic trip, we were more than ready to return to our apartment and the comforts of the known in Cusco. We arrived at the bus terminal in Cusco at 4:00 A.M. The secrets of the Incas had exhausted us.

10

Incan Creativity

Journal Entry—November 23, 2001: Today Deborah, Sophia, and Henry had plans for the day, so I decided to explore parts of Cusco I hadn't seen. I hiked up to Sacayuman and from there around the neighborhoods that are high on the hills, far from the center of town. These neighborhoods tend to be a bit rougher than the rest of Cusco. Most of the streets are of dirt, and the houses are neither as fancy nor as old as those downtown. Yet the people are as friendly as always.

I stopped at a small restaurant for an inexpensive meal around noon. There was an old woman sitting at a corner table. As I ate, she looked through me with piercing eyes. The food didn't taste quite right; that happens sometimes with inexpensive meals in Peru. As I got up to leave, the old woman said in a stern voice, "Tu no debes ser ne flojo ni perezoso. Tu debes hacer todo la que puedas." (You must not be weak or lazy. You must do all you can.) When I asked her what she meant by that, she laughed and replied, "Tu sabes. No preguntes." (You know. No questions.) Then she laughed in a weird way that left me confused, but I said, "Si, buenos tardes." (Yes, good afternoon.) And so I walked away from the restaurant and this odd encounter.

My stomach was a bit queasy and my mind was still occupied with the old woman's words, but I continued with my exploration. After some walking, I came to a deserted and open old building. I went in to have a look around. On one wall was painted a rough old mural, which showed Peruvian people dancing in front of an Incan stone palace. The paint was faded and barely recognizable. The sunlight was hitting it at strange angles. I wondered who had painted it and who once lived here. A chill ran through me, raising goose bumps all over my body.

As the sound of far-off music drifted over to my ears, the people in the painting appeared to begin moving. I became afraid and wanted to leave but felt glued to where I stood, watching the painting.

Then I believe I had a waking vision. I was in the painting with the people, who were happy to welcome my presence. They spoke to me as they danced at my side. Then all at once they weren't just people, they were the Incan Gods and Goddesses. Each swept by me with a sentence of encouragement, inspiration, or chastisement. Liviac swirled by and told me that I had to accept and assume my power.

Mama Occala floated over and said words of thanks for raising Henry and Sophia and for writing this book. Kuntur, the Condor Goddess, scratched at me with a claw and screeched "You must force your spirit to expanded and fly more." Mama Coca told me to pace myself—push, then rest.

Ch'aska, the Messenger Star, stopped and clasped my hands. I felt a warm uplifting energy spread from my hands throughout my total being. He brought me a special message: "The Gods and Goddess want you to be fully aware of your creativity and the creativity of all humans. Fill this creativity with emotions, especially burning passion, and it will allow you all to become Gods and Goddesses. You need not live boring, meaningless, or mundane lives. Put this message in your book. You must tell people of it wherever and whenever you speak. The political, business, and religious leaders of your world want people without passion or creativity—they want people whom they can control. That cannot be allowed to continue. The people must use their creativity to be all they can be!"

Then Ch'aska exploded, and I was thrown back against a wall. I stood there shaking my head. My body was tingling, and my mind was filled with unfamiliar thoughts, ideas, and emotions. It was close to how I feel when I partially awaken from a wonderful dream. The thoughts felt so foreign that I could not fully grasp them. They were like ancient, unmoving stones, mixed with the wind, existing as one thing at one time in one thought.

I got up and walked back to the picture. The sun was no longer hitting it at the same angle. I noticed for the first time a deep scratch mark and a small burn across its surface. I stared at it a bit more and prayed, asking that the Incan Gods and Goddesses bless my family. I asked for guidance, inspiration, and improved creativity, and gave thanks for the larger-than-life vision I had been given. It was getting dark so I began my hike back to our apartment, still not sure what to make of this strange and fantastic day. Even as I sit here now, hours after these events, I still don't fully understand their meaning. What are the spirits of Peru trying to tell me?

Incan and Peruvian Creativity

In the Puno area alone, it is estimated that there are still over 700 pre-Incan dances that are regularly practiced. Many of these dances have deeply ritualistic meanings. These dances are just one of the many amazing creative statement of the Peruvian people. Weaving, dance, music, painting, art, ceramics, stone working, massive landscaping, and literature are among the unique expressions of Peruvian creative outpourings. My daughter Sophia has been most struck by the creativity here. "Poppy, why doesn't the whole world know about the paintings, and ceramics, the music, the weaving, and the dancing that they do so wonderfully in Peru? The stuff here is as good if not better than anything in the United States, yet no one knows about them."

I agree with her. Most things that are produced here have a vibrant quality that perfectly captures the essence of Peruvian life, yet little of it is seen outside of Peru. Bear in mind that this is an undeveloped country. It is not a dominant culture like that of the United States, Europe, or Japan. It has nothing like the influence of China. There is neither the money nor the organization to export large amounts of Peruvian art or make it fashionable. This is true of most nonindustrialized countries. Yes, tourists bring home the occasional token piece of art as a souvenir, but Peru oozes with unique creative statements. Sadly, the trend in our world is toward homogenization. Hollywood decides the culture and the fashion. They distribute it worldwide via movies, videos, satellites, television, and now the Internet. Madison Avenue decides the fashions and what is in vogue, driving the must-have merchandise that people buy and display in their homes. Personal creative statement is all but discouraged. Being in Peru, surrounded by such an outpouring of unique high quality creativity, I can only pray that there will be room in Earth's future for these regionally unique expressions of creativity.

Music

The music of the Incas evolved very differently than in other countries. It was based on the platonic scale of D-F-G-A-C and consisted exclusively of wind and percussion instruments. Some of the ancient musical instruments are found in museums and have been conclusively dated back to 5000 years B.C.E. It is believed that animal horns and seashells, which are still used today, were in use long before the other wind instruments. It was not until the coming of the Spanish that string instruments were introduced to the Andes region.

There are many different types of wind instruments that originated in Peru. The *ocarina* is a small oval clay instrument with twelve holes. Zamponas or *siku* (we call them panpipes) come in sizes ranging from the tiny, high-pitched *chuli* to the meter-long bass *toyo*. An *aca-*

choenado is a trumpet made from the skull of a deer. A *mohuseno* is a large bamboo flute producing the deepest bass note. The *quenua*, a flute, is today usually made of bamboo of varying lengths, depending on the pitch desired. In the past, none of these instruments were made of bamboo; rather they were made of native wood, clay, or bone. There are many additional forms of pan-pipes—like wind instruments in a wide array of breathy, hypnotic, and almost otherworldly designs producing extremely unique music.

Pinkuyllu is the name of the giant flute that is played in the south of Peru. It is never played in homes or near churches. It is thought to incite competitive male energies. It is a heroic instrument, made by removing the heart from *huranhuay* poles, which is an extremely hard wood. Under the proper circumstances, the wood can be made somewhat moldable. The instrument, when completely built, is so long that the average person attempting to play has to stand on his tiptoes, stretch his neck and look up. The *mamak* is similar to the pinkuyllu, but made of mamak wood. The *wak'rapuku* is the only instrument with a deeper and more powerful tone than the pilkuyllu. It is a trumpet made from the thickest, most crooked bulls' horns. It is fitted with a silver or brass mouthpiece. These three instruments are used at communal ceremonies, for ancient war dances, during hard work, during fights between young men, at cow branding, and at bullfights. It is said that no music can penetrate deeper into the human heart than that produced by these instruments.

Special rattles, called *shalshas*, are made from goat hooves. Drums are known as *bombos*, and they are made from hollowed-out cedar or walnut, with goatskin stretched for a beating surface. *Tomboohiebiaz* are triangular drums made of local wood and llama or goat skin.

The Peruvians adapted the traditional Spanish guitar, coming up with the *charango*, which is a small five-string instrument traditionally made of an armadillo shell. Recently, because of the need for animal protection, the charangos are being constructed of wood in a similar style. The Peruvians also created the *quatro*, a type of four-string cello. More modern additions to the Andean symphony are brass instruments, violins, and harps. These add new dimensions to the ancient music but were not Incan in origination.

I have already mentioned the Quechuen singing. I have heard it compared to ancient traditional Asian singing. It is somewhat nasal, yet quite beautiful and captivating. Quechuen vocals are performed in cities, towns, and villages, as well as being widely played on radio stations across Peru. When you get on a bus or enter a restaurant, you are never sure if you will hear the South American sensation Shakira, Christina Aguilera from the United States, or traditional Quechuen music.

Literature

Peruvian literature doesn't often make it to the *New York Times* best sellers list. However, many Andean authors are highly respected across the world. Mario Vargas Llosa is perhaps the most famous. His writing is absolutely wonderful. Jose Maria Arguedas wrote *Deep River, The Singing Mountaineers*, and *Yawar Fiesta*, along with some breathtaking Quechuen poetry. Arguedas is often gloomy and can be depressing, but his writings about the Andean people and their love of nature and the Andes mountains are some of the most inspiring passages I have ever read. Ciro Aleria wrote *Golden Serpent* and *Broad and Alien Is the World*, both of which are great books in potent prose dealing with

Peru's Amazonian jungle life. Also great reads are Julio Ramon Riberyro, Alfredo Bryce Echenique, and Sergio Bambaren. *Fire from the Andes* is not to be overlooked as a great collection of short stories by Andean women. The well-known Pablo Nuruda is perhaps the best of the Chilean poets who wrote about Machu Picchu. Cesar Vallejo is considered one of Peru's best. I should also mention two great anthologies *Peru: The New Poetry* and *Peru: The Newest Poetry*.

There are two unfortunate circumstances that prevent the majority of the world from enjoying the richness of the Andean literary tradition. The first is that precious little literature from the region has been translated into English or other languages and distributed internationally. The other is that almost nothing has been written in Quechuen, for this language is the music of the Gods! Even if it were written down, I fear that translating it properly would be a difficult if not an impossible job. Even more sadly, the majestic Aymara language still does not have an agreed upon written form.

Dance

In most pre-industrialized societies, dance held a ritualistic meaning. It was often used to tell stories, memorialize events, communicate with the Gods, court a lover, celebrate an occasion, or just have fun. The Incas were no exception. Many of the Indian dances radiated their deep essences of living energies. Creativity, passion, an appreciation of life, and the ability to love deeply are some of the elements that help them achieve these impressive artistic accomplishments. This is why their dancing captures the unblinking attention of audiences to this day.

While in Cusco, I attended a dance performance with my family. We were accompanied by Joanne, an 18-year-old student from Connecticut, and by Tommy, a 20-year-old college student of Quechuen descent. I would be hard pressed to tell you who enjoyed it most. My son, Henry, spoke about the dances for over an hour, as if they were a baseball game. He was filled with questions: Why did the men wear boots in one dance, sandals in another and dresses in a third? What did it mean to dance like that? Did the Incas dance all the time? Every week? Do they still dance like that in the villages?

Our two student friends had their favorites and greatly enjoyed the entire performance. One dance somehow reminded Joanne of her mother's home cooking and how much she missed it. She took a year off between high school and college and had been traveling for four months in Latin America. Of course, she misses home and all that is familiar. One particular dance brought her to the verge of tears with nostalgia. Tommy loved the more romantic dances; they all made him very proud of his heritage. The dances also got Tommy speaking of home cooking. Tommy told us about home-cooked cuy (guinea pig). He was glad to hear that I liked the restaurant versions; however, he assured me that in his home village, the way his mother and relatives cooked it, it was a million times better.

All these Spanish conversations were stimulated by the dances. My daughter and wife also had their favorite moments and spoke of why. Sophia felt the women were not as fluid as the men and looked too pale in the stage lights. She loved the swirling dance. Deborah felt that the opportunity to experience such ancient preserved culture performed by such enthusiastic performers was golden. I wanted more when it ended. I was hungry and tired. Yet I wanted the dancing to go on and on. The costumes wcrc handmade and each represented a different region, a different era, and a different world. The steps and interactions of the dancers were hypnotizing. Usually I'm not much for dance, yet I wanted a stop-motion film so I could see each dancer's movements in each dance. One dance spoke of celebration after a harvest, another was a romantic courtship, one was of work with animals, another was about unfairness in a village. The last was just an intense whirl of color and joy and a grand finale to this intense celebration of life. I felt like I do after a great play, as if I knew the performers in a deeply personal way. They had let me see into their souls. They had become my friends. I wanted to go have some chicha with them and discuss their feelings on the dances. I have seldom if ever felt that way about a dance performance in any country.

In each region of the Andes, there are original pre-Spanish dances that are still performed regularly. To live is wonderful; to dance, exquisite; and to dance well is divine. Some of these dances are done for tourists. Some are performed at annual festivals named for Catholic saints but celebrated with pre-Incan spiritual roots and connections. Some of the dances are done only in private at intimate village or Ayllu gatherings closed to outsiders.

Weaving the Textures of Our Lives

It is inarguable that Andean weavings, as developed by the Incas and pre-Incas, were some of the greatest textile arts the world has ever seen! The inventiveness and resourcefulness of the Peruvian weavers match and often surpass the best of Egyptian and Chinese weavings.

To this day, the Andean people outside of the major cities—when they are not building or fixing their houses, and when they are not cultivating their crops or working in their fields—are usually winding or spinning their yarn or weaving all their cloths and blankets. They do this while tending or shepherding their flocks and herds, when walking down the road, or whenever they have their hands free.

There is a huge debate about whether the four corners of the loom represent the four quadrants of the universe. However, there is no question that the art of weaving, and in fact the weavings themselves, are sacred. The intent and the patterns are both used to create sacred weavings. For the Incas, the act of weaving involved taking available raw materials such as alpaca, vicuna or llama wool, and transforming it through skill, hard work, and vision. They created clothes, ponchos, and blankets to keep themselves and their loved ones warm, mark their heritage back to a specific village, and set themselves apart as individuals with skill. If you gather 100 weavers who have worked together, each can identify the other's weaving, even if the pieces seem identical to the rest of us. Which seems superior: Buying fashionable clothes produced by underpaid people half a world away, which you are sure to see others wearing, or creating your own clothes from locally produced material? There are a few cooperatives that have started up in recent years, whose main goal is to keep each village's unique organic dyeing and weaving styles alive. Each village historically had unique weaving patterns used by no other village, but of course there were regional patterns and some basic styles that were nearly universal. We were blessed to be able to spend time with the center for traditional textiles in Cusco. They work with mostly isolated Andean villages and their work of reviving and keeping the old weaving techniques alive is wonderful and inspiring. Weaving is a spiritual act of creation. Like all true acts of creation it requires a different way of thinking, a specialized view of the world.

Many people prefer alpaca wool to any other kind, but alpacas can only be raised in high altitudes. As a consequence, llama and sheep wool are used far more widely. The vicuna is a smaller, rare, and wild cousin of the llama and the alpaca. It has never been domesticated, but it has, for centuries, been caught and sheared. It has the finest wool in all the world. In the Incan times it was used solely to make the clothes of the Sapa Incas. Today, the vicuna is an endangered and protected species, so only a small number are legally caught and sheared. It is estimated that a coat made today completely of vicuna wool would be valued at least at $5000 dollars.

Andean Landscape Art

As Westerners used to the notion of planned obsolescence, it is difficult for many of us to understand the Incan view of the world. They had countless hardworking citizens whose taxes were paid by labor to the state. They viewed the mountains as a medium for painters or other artists, and they re-fashioned villages, cities, mountains, roads, and rivers as holy works of symbolic art. There were trained artist-engineers whose skills involved re-arranging massive landscapes.

In the Empire, a great number of fragile and interrelated ecosystems, sheltered by various geographies, were accompanied by an instability of climate and geology. This forced the Incas and their ancestors, over the course of thousands of years, to develop the technologies and spiritual beliefs that would enable them to live in harmony with nature. Unlike many other cultures, the Andeans developed a peculiar manner of understanding and seeing the world as a living entity of which man is only one, inseparable part.

Many people worldwide have come to Peru to hike the Inca trail. I myself have hiked it. How many of these visitors are able to view the trail for what it was: an Incan art project? It is a symphony of landscapes. Every mountain you climb and every turn of the trail reveals a wider horizon and a better view than the one before. This process goes on for days until, at last, you top the guard post that overlooks Machu Piccu. The Inca trail and Incan highways were developed not just as utilities. They were designed with beauty and form firmly in mind. The Incas thought on a much grander scale than most societies.

The grand scale on which the Incas conceived projects is borne out by the Sacred Valley. This valley was carved out by the Willcamayu River, which is today known as the Urubamba River. It runs past Machu Picchu in the east to far beyond Pisac in the west. This is an extremely fertile valley. Its importance to the Incas as a massive crop-producing region and an extension of their fair city was immeasurable. What is seldom appreciated is that it runs almost exactly parallel to the Milky Way, as the Incas saw or interpreted the constellations in the river of stars that is our galaxy. Even fewer realized that the Incas remolded most of the landscape of the Sacred Valley to reflect the constellations of the Milky Way as they saw them. What they saw in the Milky Way, they reproduced in the Sacred Valley. Much of the redesign also reflects many of the myths that were the building blocks of the Incan society.

The complete list of parallels between the Milky Way and the Sacred Valley is quite lengthy; it has been explained in detail by a few authors and touched on by others. Some of the alterations made to cities, villages, and mountains to reflect constellations and stories of myth are so apparent as to be almost incontestable.

Machu Picchu itself was designed in the shape of a humming bird. Some argue it was also designed to represent a cayman (a species of South American alligator). Wayna Picchu is a crouching puma. Cusco, it is clear, was redesigned to resemble a running puma. Phuyupatamarca and Winayhuyna resemble different types of ducks. Ollantaytambo represented an ear of corn, and the larger valley, the Tree of Life. From the ruins of Ollantaytambo, one can look across and see the mountain Pinkuylluna, clearly reshaped in the form of Wiracocha, with four-pointed hat on his head and a hand holding a blanket of presents on his back. This reminds us all to be creators in life!

I am not the first to state that our civilization has lost its eye for quality. In California, as much if not more than anywhere else, planned obsolescence is built into municipal buildings as well as homes and computers. The Incas, however, built to last! Their stone work and massive landscaping should become a new inspiration for how society should realign our values.

The Other Arts

Pottery and ceramics are arts that were well developed by many pre-conquest Andean cultures, and they are still important today. The museums of Peru overflow with classic examples of exquisite works that have survived from antiquity. The best available for purchase today are usually based on ancient designs, shapes, and motifs, although some of the modern designs are very artistic, as well.

There is a tradition of dyed and hand-carved dried gourds, which are crafted by individuals in the cities and villages in a wide variety of detail. The most intricate are impressive pieces of art. Jewelry and metal works are also direct links back to the heritage of the Incas. The works done today, especially those in gold and silver, are often breathtaking collectors' pieces.

The Spanish greatly influenced Incan painting. Once again, the churches and museums overflow with original and awe-inspiring works. Many pieces available today, both paintings and line drawings, are done in traditional Spanish and Incan styles. The city and village murals usually speak to the emotions. The cave paintings, which were created in the remote past, are uniquely Andean. The oldest feature llamas and other animals, as well as creatures that no one can decipher—possibly extraterrestrials. Long-necked statues and dolls have evolved from the Cusquenan school of painting and sculpture. The long necks are inspired by llamas. They are fairly unique and somewhat odd. Smaller stone carvings or sculptures are available and some show great workmanship. They hardly hint at the magnificence of Sacsayahuaman or Machu Picchu, but they are nice stone carvings.

Cultivating Incan Creativity

How do Peruvians rise above their state of existence and create art of such quality? Some believe it is the magnetic energies of the Andes Mountains. Some think it's because of the ley lines, which are arterial flows of the Earth's invisible energy that crisscross the country, especially in Cusco. Others believe the soil and rocks have extraterrestrial elements in them, or that the magnetism of the Andes has pulled record amounts of meteors to the area. Some believe that time's energy itself is centered here. Many believe that the isolation from the rest of the world for centuries allowed a unique artistic statement to evolve. Still others think that the mix of coast, desert, plains, mountains, and jungle, all in such close proximity, are what has inspired such creativity. I believe that the truth is a combination of all of these things.

Yet the more important question is, how can the creativity of the Andes and the Incas serve as an inspiration for those now reading this book? The Incan secrets of creativity are available to you. Each of us has the essences of the Gods and Goddesses within us. The first step to bringing it out is understanding that your life will be better if you find your own creative statement and develop it for all it is worth. If you want to take your creativity to the next step, you must find the artistic expression you most enjoy and wish to develop. You must believe that you can be creative, and then you must make time for it. Break out of your normal life in whatever way you can. Take a week-long vacation dedicated to finding or evolving your creativity. If you can't do that, dedicate a weekend away from your home. If that's impossible for financial or other reasons, then stay home alone for a week. If none of this is possible dedicate a special time each week just for your own creative impulses. Make a list of what you feel brings you the most joy when you do it. Is it dance, acting, art, watercolors, oils? Is it pottery, sculpting, carving, weaving, sewing, singing, or playing an instrument? In my case, it's writing, but there are many expressions of creativity beyond these traditional ones. If you are not sure what brings you joy, try your hand at as many things as you can and note how each makes you feel. I am weak in most of these creative expressions, but I did find out that when I'm in the right mood, creating pottery helps to releases my stress and anger. I love acting or, perhaps, I simply love an audience. The watercolors I have produced are childlike in their appearance, but they sure change my perspective as few other activities do.

Once you know your most joyous creative outlet, start playing with it. To begin with, create artistic works no one else will ever see. Do them not even for yourself to judge, but rather for the simple enjoyment of doing them. Attempt to do it 10 different ways. Before deciding to write this book, I began a novel, a satire, a political tirade, a how-to book with a co-author, a collection of poetry, an autobiography, and a novel attempting to imitate Jack Kerouac's style. I was just writing for the thrill of writing. None of it felt right, but I learned a great deal about myself, my writing, and my voice. Long before I journeyed to Peru, I kept a journal. I write my journal entries not to be read, but rather for the joy, practice, and personal growth they provide. My journals keep my creative juices flowing.

Once you have discovered and begun to play with your creative form, it doesn't hurt to read about others' styles and methods. There are tapes and workshops galore for everything from making masks (there are some great Peruvian mask makers) to designing puppets. As a writer, I have followed Julia Cameron's *Artistic Way Journal* and I have listened to Natalie Goldberg's tape *Writing Down the Bones* hundreds of times. The best advice I have heard is if you want to be a writer, you must write. Don't allow yourself to make any excuses— just write. You may be tired. Your significant other may hate you. Perhaps your kids have made a mess of the house. You have no food in the house. You are depressed. Your computer is broken. The dog ate your notebook. Your pen ran out of ink. Find another computer or another pen and a piece of paper—any paper or even a napkin will do. Sit down and write. Just write, write, write! This is true with any form of artistic statement.

Excuses kill the artistic statement. Do not allow yourself excuses. You are a terrible writer. You just write to feed your ego. No one will ever care about or read what you write. All of that doesn't matter. Don't listen to any of your own excuses! Still create in spite of all excuses. This is true of all creative statements. They will bring you joy and spiritual fulfillment. They will bring you closest to the divine force. But to become good at them, to produce anything you can be proud of, anything that will inspire others, you must become obsessed with them. I love Cusco! I love exploring Peru. But almost every second of my time there, I was thinking of getting back to my computer. I can write this part of the book this way; I can write that part of the book that way; I forgot to say this; I can improve it by changing that part; this must be the place I get to with creative statement. If you like, your art can always be the second, third, or fourth highest priority in your life. My writing comes after my family, my business, and often my farm. But I write almost every day no matter what. If I can't make the time before I go to sleep, I get up early and write or dedicate my lunch hour to writing. In Peru, I wrote an average of five to nine hours a day. I get up most days between 3:30 A.M. and 4:30 A.M. so I can write undisturbed for four or five hours before my family gets up. It is worth it to me. I hope it is to those who read this book.

Finding your creative statement will enhance your life and increase the amount of joy. It will help you to stay grounded and centered and connected to higher spiritual powers. It is so much better for every aspect of your life to actively produce art than to passively consume the "art" that we call television, or other noncreative activities that require little of you to participate. However, to be an artist of any quality, you must become an Incan warrior. The Incas were a small tribe in the Cusco valley until they decided that they could conquer the world. They persisted until they created a political, military, and social system with no precedent in South America or in world history. The full effects of what that set in motion is still to be experienced by the planet Earth. You too, have that much potential in you. If you decide to make an artistic statement and then promise yourself to continue working with it no matter what, then your creative expressions will improve the whole world. Try it, and you'll see that it's true.

Peru is mystery personified, not just for me but for anyone who becomes interested in it! I have traveled quite a bit in my life but no country I have ever been to feels so unique, so magical, and so other-worldly. Peru today is an outgrowth of countless ancient mysteries, and we have only fractured records of what and who they were. These mysteries and the creativity we have spoken about can greatly help us function better in today's challenging world.

11

Incan Living—The Archetypical Inca Trail

Journal Entry—December 6th, 2001: We are on a bus returning from a wonderful nine-day trip to Ariquipa, the Colca Canyon, Tacna, and northern Chile. It was another amazing, heavenly trip. We met many wonderful and friendly people and saw such awesome places and things.

In Ariquipa we saw Juanita, the 500-year-old frozen Ice Maiden mummy. We also visited a 400-year-old nunnery, where one of the late Sisters is being considered for sainthood because of feats such as telepathy and teleportation. Her spirit supposedly still appears to people in need today.

In Colca Canyon we found Incan terraces that are more extensive than imaginable. The canyon is deeper and more beautiful than the Grand Canyon. As we viewed it, fourteen condors flew closely over our heads. We even had our pictures taken with an Andean eagle on each of our shoulders.

Tacna has great wine. Northern Chile as a whole was wonderful. We saw the highest non-navigable lake in the world, some of the grandest volcanoes anywhere, and ancient Inca-founded villages that are still occupied. We saw ruins, mummies, and pictoglyphs that all date back over 5,000 years! Part of the Tiwanaku federation? Our hotel in Arica had been overbooked because there were many stranded tourists in town due to an airline strike. We ended up staying at the hotel owners' beachfront mansion for four days. The four of us had this glorious mansion all to ourselves! We felt like royalty. The hot Chilean beaches were a pleasant break from cool Cusco.

As we bounce back to Cusco on this bus, I wonder why? Why are we so lucky? Why does everything seem to work out so well *for us? Luck is a portion of the answer. I know that the Incan Gods and Goddesses are guiding and protecting us. I am also thankful to say that my family has adapted a wonderful approach to life. We don't seem to approach it as do many other people or families. To sum it up simply yet understandably, we love and respect each other and all are committed to helping each other learn, evolve, and enjoy life. We all expect the best in life and are willing to plan and prepare to make that happen. We are all adaptable, and when things aren't quite right we work together to make the most of them. That sounds too good to be true. It isn't true 100 percent of the time, but more than not we live the Incan life! We have become much better at doing that in South America and I can now better understand and explain what that means.*

Attitude of the Incas

We are living in challenging times, to say the least. To deal with our daily challenges, we must consciously cultivate our creative expressions, mindfulness, and common sense, in addition to making the commitment to self-improvement and to unselfishly helping others. All of these are important elements of living the Incan life. We must also use discretion in listening to the media and about what we choose to believe. We must all remember that answers are not as simple as the mass media makes them seem. As I write these words, the world has witnessed some of the strangest events in recent decades. There are those of us who believe that the media, in particular, are capitalizing on negative news in order to keep people locked into their roles as fearful and helpless victims.

Without question, life can be depressing and some-times even overwhelming. If you have no job, no money, and no food, or if you or your loved ones are threatened with death from disease, war, or terrorist attacks, then it's more than challenging to believe in a golden future. It's more than challenging to re-dedicate yourself to all the elements of living the Incan life.

But in truth, there is no better time than now. Pachacuteq, the most famous of all the Sapa Incas, rose to power and revolutionized the Andes region and all its people; his impact and inspiration is still being felt today. It is instructive to note that this happened when the Incan Empire was at what was, until then, its lowest point. Pachacuteq saw his father and brother, the chosen heir, flee Cusco to hide, thereby allowing the Chancas to have all that their ancestors had built. He took a difficult stand, risking his very life to stand and say, "I believe we Incas can defend our valley and our heritage." Pachacuteq won the day! One legend has it that the rocks of Cusco themselves were so inspired by his determination that they rose up beside him and helped win the war.

What this legend tells us is that our dark days will also pass. Life will assist us when we decide to dedicate ourselves to a better tomorrow. There are no great people in history—Inca, Peruvian or otherwise—who did not suffer setbacks, great disappointments, and defeats. Victory does not go to the weak and fearful. Victory does not go to those who give up.

The Inca Trail

I have come to believe that there are two Inca Trails—the one from Ollantaytambo in the Sacred Valley to Machu Picchu, and a second archetypical, mythical Inca Trail. This second one represents the difficult challenges of choosing to live the magical life of an Incan warrior. Each

Inca Trail is about the difficulty of climbing each upcoming mountain. On the archetypical mythical trail, you face mental, physical, and spiritual challenges, the likes of which you could never have anticipated. But each view from the mountain pass is more unimaginable glorious than the one before. In the Sacred Valley, the physical Inca Trail gives you a unique reward—the city of Machu Picchu, a place my children say is like nothing they have ever experienced. I have to agree with them and the 360,000 people who visit it year after year.

On the archetypical Inca Trail, to which I ask you to dedicate your life, the choices seem simple but are far from it. You can live an unfulfilling life, work at an unfulfilling job, watch television, and avoid truly living day and night and all weekend long, thereby wasting the most precious gift in the whole universe—your life. In mountain climbing, those who choose that life are comparable to those who either never begin the climb or those who give up along the way and go home before they reach the top. I am a camper and a backpacker. I have spent weeks, soaking wet and cold and physically exhausted, wondering what I was doing and why. Yet I persisted. Those have been some of the most rewarding and most memorable adventures in my life.

I will always remember canoeing down the Merrimac River with David Himmer and Gene Kettlehorn, two of my all-time best adventure buddies. We heard the roar of a waterfall that wasn't on our map. David turned to us and said, "We can go ashore and turn the canoe around or we can take our chances. But the difference between doing something and not doing it is just doing it!" We agreed. Gene put his guitar in plastic and tied it down. We paddled for all we had in us, right over the waterfall. It was a rough waterfall and we capsized. We almost drowned, and maybe by rights we should have. But we survived. We retrieved our beat-up canoe, gear, and paddles, swam to shore and laughed our fool heads off. I have told that story so often I have worn it out, but in my life it was a turning point. I learned the difference between backing off when you are afraid and giving your best effort. My life has been so fulfilling because I always attempt to push the envelope and just do whatever I'm doing to the best of my abilities. I tackle whatever challenge is put in front of me, and when there is no challenge, I tend to create one or at least raise my goals. For me that is the archetypical Inca Trail and there is no better time to embark upon it than right now.

We have Pachacuteq's example. When everything around us is in turmoil and everyone is disenchanted and talking about the end of the world, that's the time to dig in and make a plan to take whatever actions we can to improve our lives and the lives of all those we touch. It is up to each of us to assist in the building of the Golden Age that Earth and humanity deserve. We Incan warriors must commit our lives to climbing the Inca Trail, until, together, we reach the best possible future. The trials and turmoil of today are but opportunities for all of us to push our limits and improve our lives.

Suggestions for Beginning to Climb the Archetypical Inca Trail

Heart

Incan living is first about heart. If we can learn to live in love we can embrace our fullest selves and assist others to do the same. Love is the most powerful force in the whole universe! If we feel unloved, then what we need to do is find others who feel unloved and help them. Love is not measured by what we receive but by how much we give.

Quality of Life

Most lives are mere shadows of their fullest potential. We are subtly taught from childhood that we are helpless victims, that we never have enough love, money, time, or energy. Just never enough of anything. Well, the truth is we are all limitless aspects of the Gods. We can have enough of whatever we believe we deserve.

Enthusiasm

The first key to success in any endeavor is to bring enthusiasm to it. Whether it's washing dishes or filing papers, enthusiasm makes all the difference. If you don't have enthusiasm, there are simple ways to help bring it into you life. The simplest way is to make enthusiasm in and of itself your goal. Act as enthusiastically as you can until it starts becoming your real state of being.

Passion

As with enthusiasm, life is only worth living if you are passionate about whatever you are doing. People's lives should only be lived in one way—in a constant state of passion. This should become a burning goal.

Creativity

In most peoples' lives, there are too few really creative outlets. Our work should have creativity in it. So should our hobbies. It can be cooking or gardening or mechanics. It is important for everyone to have a creative hobby and spend time each week on it, for people are closest to breaking free of life's restrictions when they let their creativity flow into every aspect of their waking day.

A Dream, A Vision

Everyone should have a dream or a vision of what they want their lives to be. Retirement is not a self-empowering dream. However, traveling the world is a great dream, and being the best at whatever you do is another. People are afraid to dream big. It is much better to aim at the stars and hit the moon than it is to aim at a sparrow and hit only a rock.

Imagination

In the universe, there is only one limit and that is our imagination. Whatever you can conceive, you can achieve. Everything that exists in the world existed first in the imagination of some person. Use and stretch yours whenever possible.

Work

We are taught from childhood to aspire to high-paying jobs. The problem is that many high-paying jobs pay so well because they slowly devour your soul. Big businesses often desire soulless robots on their payrolls. It is far better to honestly decide how you love to spend your time and then pursue that, regardless of the financial compensation. If you love it, your work will feed your soul and allow you to feed the souls of all you touch. In truth, this is much more valuable then any six- or seven-digit annual salary.

Family and Close Friends

Family and friends are both funny words. These words can mean the people that share your blood, who share your life. These words can mean the people you are closest to, a bond of love, a bond of security. We owe it to ourselves at some point in our lives to examine all our relationships. The ones that give back to us more than or as much as they take are the ones we should recommit to, nurture, and savor. The ones that we have outgrown or that have become negative, and the ones that consistently take more than they give are those that we can attempt to alter or heal. If we can't heal them after reasonable effort, then we need to cut loose and run from them. Removing parasites and negative people from our lives is not always easy, but it is extremely empowering and essential to personal growth. This doesn't apply to our children— although we all have fantasies of doing that (especially with teenagers). It doesn't apply to our elderly sick parents who loved and supported us throughout our lives. When you have an obligation, you must fulfill it. In most cases, family and friends should be the people you love, who nurture you. They should be your strongest support system. If they are not, you should set that, too, as a goal and take actions to build healthy relationships.

Activities We Love

Drinking alcohol, smoking dope, shopping, gambling, and other forms of substance abuse are only an escape. Fixing cars, collecting stamps, horseback riding, volunteering to assist those less fortunate than you, gardening, and backpacking are examples of activities you love that feed your soul in healthy ways. They recharge you, light you up, and expand your level of joy. Activities you love are often what you do when you aren't getting paid or being responsible. The more of your time you can give to these loving areas, the healthier you will be.

Magic

All these things mentioned, if done well, are magic. Done in a complementary symphony, they become totally synergetic which means that the life they weave is even more than the equivalent of its wonderful parts added together. Thus a magical life is not only achievable, magical Incan living is the only way to live! We can and we must overcome the odds! We must dedicate our lives to climbing the archetypical Inca Trail. The final destination is worth all the effort.

12

Summing It Up—Epilogue

Journal Entry—December 27th, 2001: *We are at the airport in Lima again. We have passed through some particularly rigorous customs, and now await our departure back to the States and our old lives.*

Our four months in Peru just flew by; none of us wanted to leave. Henry best summed up our feelings. He lives for sports—especially baseball, but the day before Christmas, he said, "I would give up baseball if we could stay longer or come back like this again." Sophia showed some of her Cusco friends how to use e-mail at the cyber cafes and signed them up for Yahoo. She promised Jaime, her quenua (pronounced kena, ancient Incan flute) teacher, that she would continue practicing, take more lessons, and always play it proudly.

Deborah has finished writing a great book on the importance of foreign-born, adopted children to live in the land of their birth for a prolonged time to positively effect their self-image and confidence. I swear that if the Peruvian people can be so happy, hard working, loving, and friendly in spite of all the odds against them, then I will do more in my life with all the opportunities I have been given. As for me, I am almost finished with my book, but it will never truly stop for me. This book is just another step in fulfilling the promise I made to the Incan Gods and Goddesses.

As we wait to leave Peru, we are all sad. However, we know we will return and we also know that these four months have touched us and changed something in us—it has made us different people. The children swear they are going to give away most of their toys and old clothes to people who need them more. As a first step, we left all but two changes of clothes each to the street people of Cusco.

We spent Christmas Eve in Cusco. Deborah and the children went to sleep at 11 P.M., but I stayed up and went to the cathedral in the Plaza de Armas to see a portion of the midnight mass. At midnight, I walked out in front of the church to see fireworks and bonfires all over the plaza and all over the mountains that surround Cusco. It was one unimaginable display of fireworks, all shot off by the people themselves—the city sponsors none of it. As I watched, I cried like a baby. To be leaving Cusco and Peru and South America is heartbreaking. It is so hard to leave all the great times and all our new and wonderful friends. I also cried for the suffering and struggle of these noble people. And I cried because I was just so thankful for the gift of having a great four months in Peru with my family. I hate to leave but I am nothing but grateful for all I have been given. I hope I will be able to share some of what I have experienced and learned with many others. Viva la Peru! May we all live the best we can as the Incas did. Many of their secrets will allow us to.

Now and Then

There is a higher vibration rising from Peru. It is early morning and the birds are making beautiful music. There is a mist in the air as a family rises to greet the day. They have potato soup heated on the fire for breakfast. They dress in traditional garb and leave the house to check on the llama and alpaca herd along with their crops. This could be a scene from 2000 B.C.E. or today in some of the isolated villages of the Peruvian Andes.

Many families left the mountains because of civil wars, poverty, and the desire for all things modern. Lima is bursting at her seams. However, there are many families who have chosen to stay or have even left for the big cities and returned to live in the way of their ancestors. Peru is a country with a vast yet mysterious history overflowing with mysteries and secrets. The Incan Empire was the culmination of thousands of years of ever-advancing cultures that developed in the Andes. The Incas are estimated to have existed only from 1100 C.E. until 1533 C.E.—the blink of an eye in the history of human civilization—yet under their Empire, more people and land were united than in most other societies the world has ever seen.

There are countless beautiful aspects of the Incan culture, chief among them its very existence. As I have stated, the Incas believed in a strong ruling class, and the consequences for going against that pattern were harsh. However, the Incan laws were few; be honest and work hard was what most of them were about. It was a loose federation of villages based on a compassionate centralized government. The glue that held it all together was the premise that today I will help you, and tomorrow you will help me. The Incan highway connected most of the Empire, no matter how remote. Relay runners swiftly moved news and messages from one end of the Empire to the other. They had no riding animals and only minimal understanding or use of anything resembling the wheel, yet many of their structures were built so well that they remain standing today, still inspiring tourists, academics, and writers alike.

The Incan views of spirit and the secrets of life were extremely different from that of our present day outlook. There was not one dominant culture, but rather a patchwork quilt of many traditions, much knowledge and many beliefs. As far as we can tell, these were shared and taught basically through experience and the oral tradition.

The Incas understood how to work with nature as an ally, not as some chaotic force to be conquered. They saw and acted from within, with a clear understanding of their symbiotic role with nature. There existed a world view that saw our planet as a place of dreams. By viewing the world as a place of dreams, there was a wisdom that, through working in harmony with nature, with intent, will, and hard work, all of life could and often was transformed.

The secrets of time and space were not available to every shepherd. However, there was a sense of deeper understanding available for anyone who woke up and decided they wanted more from their lives. Each individual had value, as well as the freedom to fulfill his or her potential, and the understanding that all are connected in a tight web of life.

There were truths then that the Incas knew, which we would be well served to remember. These truths tell us that, together, the love, caring and joy we share makes us all part of the Gods and Goddesses. We are aspects of Pacha Mama. We are the dreamers and the dream. We exist to savor the experience of living with the limitations of time and place, full in the consciousness that, even if we are lucky, we will have not very many decades of life. The Incas understood that and they embraced it fully. We too must live every moment to its fullest.

Many of the mysteries and secrets of the Incas might have been lost forever. However, many threads, relics, and legends point us to the secrets they knew. In many villages, the traditions of the Incas have been passed down in a continuum of tradition. Nothing, not even the Spanish conquest, the spread of Christianity, or the modern invasion of Western culture, has been able to destroy all of the Incas' secrets or knowledge.

For those of us who live today, this is most important. There was a belief among some Incas of the past that humanity would reach a time when it would no longer be limited in the ways it had been until then. Our perceptions of reality would shift and broaden. Our senses and abilities would expand. The barriers between humans and nature would lessen and the veils between dimensions would become simpler to penetrate. Many believe that this time is coming and will be here in the next two decades. It has been said that in order to help in this great time of change, the secrets of the Incas must be brought to the light of day, so that their unique knowledge will show humanity how to reach our highest potential. We do not have to be wage slaves any more. We do not have to have a holy man to talk to God for us. We do not have to allow our lives to be controlled. It is the time for each individual to begin to realize they have the power to set themselves free and live joyous, meaningful, and fulfilling lives.

There is much for us to learn from the descendants of the Incan people and their most recent five centuries of loss and suffering. They had years of joy before the Spanish came. That was their time of growth and expansion. The world they crafted was like no other in the world before or since. Then Pizzarro came and ended their dream. However, there is a certain indefinably special quality about today's Quechuen people, the proud descendants of the Incas. It is not only their lungs and spleens that are bigger than those of most other people; on many levels, their hearts are bigger as well.

The Quechuen capacity for love and caring is something the rest of the world can and should learn from. There are important lessons here for all of us: Dignity under pressure. Love in spite of continuous abuse. In European terms, it is a kind of alchemy which makes gold out of lead. If you are handed lemons then make the best lemonade you can. There are those Peruvian people who call the last five centuries simply the time of suffering and pain. They believe it existed to prepare the descendants of the Incas for what is coming. If we all do our best, a new world will follow that will be a Golden

Age on Earth. A time when the best of what the Incas knew is brought forth to the world.

One definition of happiness is enjoying what you have and working to improve it. The planet Earth is at a crossroads. It is never too late to undo our mistakes. The Incas once had something close to an ideal state based on love, compassion, and fairness to all. The Peruvians today understand love, inclusiveness, the importance of taking risks, and of making decisions based on your heart, not just logic. If the Earth and all of humanity is destined to achieve a golden age where people take back their power and begin again to make their own personal decisions while expressing their creativity and joy, then we need a huge influx of Incan wisdom. Their past was not nor is their present perfect, but Peru offers the world a great many possible ways to improve society. I pray that this book can reach a wide audience and open their hearts to the alternative Incan and Peruvian possibilities. The future belongs to those brave enough to risk change and strong enough to begin living creatively from their hearts.

Let's all start believing in a better day and working towards co-creating it. Let's all embrace this as Incan warriors! The secrets of the Incas are countless; one of the most important is that each of us can and will make a magical difference with every thought, word, and action we take.

The secrets of the ancient Incas and life in Peru are the most delicious and potent foods I have tasted in the world. They are burning and sweet. They radiate happiness. Being in Peru and exploring the writings and teachings about the Incas has been like drinking sunlight on a regular basis. To the Incas, the Andes, the Amazon, and to Peru, I extend my deepest gratitude for what they have given me and my family, and for what they are offering all humanity.

Glossary

Quechuen and Spanish Terms

Acha—Chica, homemade Peruvian corn beer

Aclla—Chosen women

Alto Mesayoq—Shaman who stands at the apex of the religious hierarchy and communicates with native deities and the spirits of the dead.

Ati—Power

Amaru—A spiritual force that upsets the apple cart and brings about a new equilibrium.

Apu—The Goddesses and Gods that live in and are the mountain peaks. They protect and punish the people they look over.

Awsancate—Sacret mountain near Cusco

Ayahuasca—Hallucinogentic plant. In Quechuen it literally means "The vine of the dead."

Ayawaskeros—Healers who work with Ayahuasca

Ayllu—Andean community, ancient extended neighborhood with traditional ties

Ayni—Andean reciprocal system of shared labor and goods

Brujo—Magic worker/witch

Brujeria—Magic or witchcraft

Callawayakuna—Bolivian healer

Caypacha—Andean world of humans, planets, animals, minerals

Ccoricenci—Mythical bird of wisdom

Ceque—Radial ritual line on the landscape surrounding Cusco and other Incan settlements; Incan version of laylines

Ch'allascca—Ritual to begin harvest

Chicha—Incan beer made from corn

Chompa—A knitted sweater C'intu—rituals to the Apus using coca leaves

Conopa—Domestic sacred entities; usually carved out of stone in the shape of a llama, alpaca, maize or potatoes

Coraconcha or Qorikancha—Main Cusco Sun Temple

Cuca acllay—Ritual of reading the future in coca leaves

Cuca C'intu—A ritual offer of coca leaves

Curak Aculleq—Highest level of initiated Andean master

Coye or cuy—Guinea pig

Curandero—Folk healer

Enchantodor—Enchanter

Ghoque—Gold in natural state

Hallpay—Ritual or everyday act of chewing coca leaves

Haywaricuy—Offering, meaning "to reach the Earth"

Haywascca—Blessing or prayer

Hechiceria—Sorcery

Hechicero—Sorcerer

Hechizo—Spell

Huaca—Sacred entity or energies usually in the form of a natural object or place.

Huacacamayo—Minister or caretaker of deities

Huacapvillac—Interpreter of Huaca's communications

Huanca—Usually a large stone or natural setting where ancestor spirits reside

Illa—Rock or stone shaped like an animal

Incaychus—Personal amulets that come from the apus and contain a life-force to prevent sickness

Inti Raymin—Festival of the Sun, celebrated in June in Cusco

Intiwantana—The tying up of the sun, a stone pillar in many Incan ceremonial sites

Iwayllu—Supernatural, mythical animal

Lacicca—Native Incan religious specialist

Laycca—Female Peruvian healer

Machu michuycuna—Ancient beings

Malliqui—Mummified corpse, bones or other remains of ancestors of ayllu. In pre-Spanish times, these were treated as living beings. The witch trials and Inquisition had most of them burned and the practice successfully stopped.

Mago—Wizard

Mosccoycuna—Dreams

Munayniyuk—In Andean mythology, one with the gift of love

Obraje—Weaver

Orejon—Spanish name for Incan nobles because of the huge earplugs they wore, literally "big ears"

Oro y quri—Gold that has been worked by human hands

Pacca or **Piccocuna** or **Pama mesayoq**—Andean herbalist, performer of rituals

Paqparina—Place of origin of each Ayllu

Qoyllur R'iti—Annual sacred Pervian pilgrimage, in which at least one person dies each year

Quipu-kamayoc—Masters of the knotted cords

Rumasimi or Run simi—Original name for Quechuen language, meaning "the peoples' tongue"

Runa—People, humans

Sapa Intiq Churin—Sapa Inca, only son of the Sun

Sorocckkch'e—Altitude sickness, usually curable by drinking coca tea and resting; however, in serious cases a person has to travel to lower altitudes

Sortilego—Divination, diviner

Sullu—Fetus of a llama or alpaca used in modern-day rituals and divine offerings

Suyu alto misayoq—Andean healer who administers to an entire region

Tambo—Transit point on the Inca highway

Taki Onqoy—Dance of disease; native religious revivalist movement; a movement that flourished in the area of Huamanga in 1565 CE.

Tawantinduyu—The Incan Empire; four quarters, four directions, or four regions joined together

Ukha Pacha—Underworld or inner world

Unuchacuy—Andean ritual for initiates

Usna—Tiered platform where the Incan elite stood during ceremonies

Waca—Sacred place or object or shrine

Wac'arumi—Sacred stones

Wanuy—Death

Willca—Andean tree, hallucinogenic powder was made from it and inhaled through one's nose in ritual

Yachac—Person of knowledge

Yachayniyucc—One with the gift for learning

Incan and South American Gods and Goddesses

Amaru—Incan snake God

Ai Apaec—Supreme God of Moche

Apocatequal—Chief priest of Incan Moon Goddess; also for the Goddess Lighting

Apu Yaaya Jesucristo—Apu Jesus Christ

Apu Punchau—Another name for Inti, or an Apu

Ataguchu—Incan God who assisted in Creation

Axo Mama—Incan potato Goddess

Catequil—God of Thunder and Lightning

Ccoa—Puma Spirit Goddess of Kuri, Peru

Chasca Coyallar—God of Flowers, protector of maidens

Chaski, Ch'aska, or Chasa—Incan messenger; star, Venus, the planet with smoking hair. The Goddess represented by the evening star, the morning star, and the dawn.

Chia—Goddess of Moon and Music in Colombia

Chochonyi—Chilean God of Nightmares

Coca Mama—Incan Coca Goddess

Copacati—Guardian God of Lake Titicaca

Cuarancy—Brazilian God who created animals

Hanan Pacha—Gods of the after-life realm

Huacas—Incan tribal Gods

Huaillepenyi—Chilean Fog God

Ihuaivulu—Volcano Goddess

Illapa—Thunder and Lightning God

Kay Pacha—Earth

Keri and **Kama Oka**—The twins who were the Goddess of the Puma and Jaguars

Keyeme—Lord of Animals

Kurupira—Brazilian God that protects animals

K'uychi—Rainbow God

Maive-Monan—Brazilian God of agriculture and laws

Mama Allpa—A second Earth Goddess, more a fertility and nurturing Goddess who was depicted with multiple breasts

Mama Chucha—Uruguayan God of underground treasures

Mama Occala—Ocean, Sea and Water Goddess

Mama Quilla or Killa Mama or Pacsa Mama—Moon Goddess

Mero—Mother of Pumas

Meuler—Chilean God of whirlwinds and Typhoons

Pachacamac—Sea God lover of Pacha Mama and brother of Viraconca and Manco Capac

Pache Mamma—The Incan Earth Mother

Phaway—Condor God

Perdu—Brazilian God of human reproduction

Pihcechenyi—Chilean (Araucanian) demon

Punchau—Another name for Inti

Qocha Mama—Mother and Sea Goddess

Sach'a Mama—Mother tree or the tree of life

Si—Chimo Moon God

Supi—Gods of death and the underworld

Tejeto—Fire bringer; God of Caingang of Brazil

Thoka Nkas—Holy place

Turner de Mazie—Corn Bore God

Wiracocha, Viacocha, or Wiraqocha; Illateqsi, Tunupa, Inkariy; or alternatively Illa Tica Uira-Cocha—Incan Creator God

Yakumama—Mother Water Goddess

Bibliography

Magazines

Cuandernos Andinos Magazine. 2001, 13, Cusco, Peru.

Magical Blend Magazine. 2001. Chico, California.

Natural Beauty and Health. 2001. Chico California.

Tampu Magazine of Andean Culture. 2001. 2, May, Cusco, Peru.

Via Lactea Magazine. August 2000. Cusco, Peru.

Books

Arguedas, Jose Maria. 1958. *Deep Rivers*, Austin, Texas: University of Texas Press.

Asher, Robert. 1982. *Code of the Quipu.* Lansing Michgan: University of Michgan Press.

Bingham, Hiram. 1989. *Lost City of the Incas.* Lima, Peru: Ediciones Turisticas.

Brown, Michael E. 1986. *Tsewa's Gift.* Washington, D.C. and London: Smithsonian Institute.

Childress, David Hatcher. 1986. *Lost Cities and Ancient Mysteries of South America.* Stelle, Illinois: Childress Adventures Unlimited Press.

Clessen, Constance. 1993. *Inca Cosmology and the Human Body*. Salt Lake City, Utah: University of Utah Press.

Cumes, Carol, and Valencia, Romulo Lizarraga. 1995. *Journey to Machu Piccu*. St. Paul, Minnesota: LLewellyn Publications, St. Paul.

Escalante, Javier M. 2001. *Tiwanaku Guide Book*. La Paz, Bolivia: Editorial Presencia.

Frost, Peter. 2000. *Exploring Cusco*. Lima, Peru: Nuevas Imagenes, S.A.

Griffiths, Nicholas. 1995. *The Cross and the Serpent*. Norman, Oklahoma: University of Oklahoma Press.

Kauffmann-Dojg, Federico. 2001. *Sex in Ancient Peru*. Lima, Peru, Merkatus.

Keatinge, Richard W. 1999. *Peruvian Prehistory*. Cambridge, UK: Cambridge University Press.

Hemming, John. 1993. *The Conquest of the Incas*. London: Macmillan.

Hurtado, Manual Huanqui, and Condorena, Milton Montufar. 2000. *Cusco Magnetico*. Cusco, Peru: Altelier Pauqarwasi.

Markham, Sir Clements. 1977. *The Incas of Peru*. Lima, Peru: ABC.

Moseley, Michael E. 1997. *The Incas and Their Ancestors*. New York: Thames and Hudson.

Merejildo Chaski, James Are'valo. 1997. *The Awakening of the Puma*. Cusco, Peru: Chaski.

Metraux, Alfred. 1969. *The History of the Incas*. New York: Schocken Books.

Patchett, Ann. 2001. *Bel Canto*. New York: HarperCollins Publishing.

Poman, Human. 1978. *Letter to a King*, translated by Christopher Dilke, New York: E.P. Dutton.

Prescott, William. 1847. *Conquest of Peru.* New York: HarperCollins Publishing.

Prescott, William H. 1900. *Peru in Two Volumes.* New York: Peter Fenelon Collier & Son.

Rachowiecki, Rob. 2000. *Peru.* Lima, Peru: Lonely Planet.

Salazar, Fernando E. Elorrieta, and Salazar, Edgar Elorrieta. 2001. *Cusco and the Sacred Valley of the Incas.* Cusco, Peru: Tanpus S.R.L.

Salazar, Fernando E. Elorrieta, and Salazar, Edgar Elorrieta. 1996. *The Saced Valley of the Incas, Myths and Symbols.* Cusco, Peru: Sociedad Pacasitanpu Hatha.

Savoy, Gene. 1970. *Antisuyo.* New York: Simon and Schuster.

Sullivan, William. 1986. *The Secret of the Incas.* New York: Crown Publishing

Urton, Gary. 1999. *Inca Myths,* London: The Trustees of British Museumns.

de la Vega, Garcilaso. 1979. *The Royal Commentaries of the Incas.* Lima, Peru: ABC Original.

Valderrama, Escalante, Gelles and Martinez. 1996. *Andean Lives.* Austin, Texas: University of Texas Press.

Villoldo, Alberto, 2000, Shaman, Healer, Sage, New York, Random House.

Wilkins, Harold T. 1998. *Secret Cities of Old South America.* Kempton, Illinois: Adventures Unlimited Press.

Write, Ronald, and Callanupa, Nilda. 1998. *Quechua Phrasebook.* Oakland, California.: Lonely Planet.

Index

A

Acachoenado, 164–65
Aclla, 38–39
Adoption:
 in Peru, 48–50
 in U.S., 46–49
Affirmations, 67
Aleria, Ciro, 166–67
Aligning vision, 60–62
Allies:
 calling, 69
 death and the dead as,
  116–18
 finding, 67–69
Alpacas, 171
Altar, 95
Altiplano, 29–30
Amaru, Tupac, 20–21
Amaute, 37
Amazon, 30–31, 55, 78,
 194
Ancestor worship, 116–18
Ancestral gods, 42–43
Andahahuaylillas, 145–46
Andean landscape art,
 171–73
Andean priest, 120

Andes, 10, 29–30, 65, 78,
 169, 174, 191, 194
 spraying of chica into
  subsoil, 119
Animal spirits, 65
Apartment rental, in
 Cusco, 75–76
Apus, 42–43, 56, 122
Ara, 95, 98
Archetypical Inca Trail:
 activities we love,
  186–87
 beginning to climb,
  183–87
 creativity, 184–85
 dream/vision, 185
 enthusiasm, 184
 family/close friends,
  186
 heart, 183
 imagination, 185
 magic, 187
 passion, 184
 quality of life, 184
 work, 185
Arguedas, Jose Maria, 166
Ariquipa, 179
Astral spirit, 70–71

Astral travels, 143–44
  fear during, 144
  Incan technique for,
    143–44
  of spiritual Incas, 87
Astrology, and the Incas,
  44
Astronomy, and the Incas,
  44
Attahualpa, 35
Aura, 70–71
Ayahuasca, 91–92
Ayllu, 38, 107, 130
  worship of founders of,
    42
Aymara language, 167
Aztecs, 41

B

Balancing the oppositional
  forces in Incan lives,
  42
Bambaren, Sergio, 167
Bay leaves, 100
Bear, as symbol of the
  Earth, 123
Bolivia, 149–59
Bombos, 165
Boric Ruz Explorer
  Organization, and
  searches for
  treasure, 85
Brass instruments, 166
Burros, 78

Burton, Richard, 76

C

Calvairio, 150
Canchis Province, 146
Casa Serana, 45
Catholic Church, 84–85
  and Ayllu beliefs, 43–44
Cave paintings, 174
Ceramics, 173–74
Ceremonial candles, 96,
  101
Ceremonies, 67
Chachapoyas culture, 29
Chakras, 70–71
Ch'ally, 118
Chamomile, 100
Chanca tribe, 33
Charangos, 153, 166
Chariots of the Gods (von
  Daniken), 155
Ch'aska (Inca messenger),
  15, 25, 162
Chaven (Warrior God),
  113
Chavene (Weeping
  Goddess), 113
Chavez, Ruben, 76
Chavin culture, 29
Chica, 18, 43
Chicken feather, 100
Chimu culture, 29
Chinchero, 107–9
Chosen of the Sun, 38

Chupas, 148
Chuqui Yllayllapa
  (Thunder God), 15,
  23, 112
Church of Miracles, 150
Clay water vessel, 100
Coca, 43
Coca leaves, 100, 121–22
Colca Canyon, 179
Colla tribe, 147–48
College years, 10
Commitment, 46–47
Communion (Striber),
  155
Compromise, 23–26
Condor feather, 100
Condor Goddess
  (Kuntur), 112
Condors, 65
Condors throne, 21–23
Copacabana, 149–51
Coraconcha, 36, 85–86
Corn, and the Incas, 29
Corn Goddess (Sara
  Mama), 43
Corn Worm God (Kuru),
  114
Coya, queen of the Incas,
  17
Creativity, 184–85
Creator God, 15, 18, 24,
  31–32, 33, 111
Culture, of the Incas, 9, 27,
  28–29, 79–80, 191
Curanderos, 140

Curendarios, 84
Cuscaniane Sistine
  Chapel, 146
Cusco, 55–57, 61, 67, 75,
  159, 168, 173, 174,
  179–80
  apartment rental in,
    75–76
  rainy night in, 79–80
  and searches for
    treasure, 85
Cusco Valley, 32, 34, 36
Cusquenan school of
  painting and
  sculpture, 174
Cuy, 18

D

Dance/dancing, 19–20,
  130, 153–54, 165,
  167–69
Death of family/friends,
  in a dream, 22
Death penalty, 39–40
Deceased animal
  companions, spirits
  of, 65
Dedication of life to the
  Gods and
  Goddesses, 22
Despachos, and home
  blessing, 119
Disks of the sun, 85–86
Diviners, 37

Dragonflies, 68
Dream journal, 135–36
Dreams, 14–18, 20, 22,
    24–26, 185
  defined, 135
  exercise to control, 135
  Incan, 133–44
Drums, 165

E

Earth Goddess (Pacha
    Mama), 15, 24–25,
    43, 56, 60–61, 111,
    123, 130, 133, 154,
    193
Echenique, Alfredo Bryce,
    167
"El Condor Pasa", 78
El Patio, 45
Emotional energies,
    65–67
Enthusiasm, 184
Ethereal body, 70–71

F

Family/close friends, 186
Fasting, and rituals, 121
Fear, and negative allies, 69
Fertility Goddess (Mama
    Hanka), 113–14
Fighting Spanish
    conquistadors, in a
    dream, 20–21

Fire spirits, 68
First magical staff, 93–102
Flute-like wind
    instruments, 153
Flutes, 165
  in ritual work, 100
Fujimori, Alberto, 52–53
Future storytelling, 66–67

G

Genito, Deborah, *See*
    Langevin, Deborah:
Gentil Mach ancestor
    worship, 116–18
Goal setting, 76–77
Gods and Goddesses, *See*
    Incan Gods and
    Goddesses
Goldberg, Natalie, 176
Golden Age on Earth,
    192–93
Golden disks of the sun,
    85–86
Guanocvicuna (Llama
    God), 113
Guevera, Che, 10, 18
Gurries, Victor, 134

H

Harps, 166
Harvest rituals, 87
Hatumpi ccatu or
    despacho, 95, 97

Healers, 83–84, 140
Heart, 183
Hidden treasures, stories
    of, 84–85
High Priest, 36–37
Himmer, David, 183–84
Hitchhiking to Miami, 11
Home blessing, 118–20
    "Wasi hun'ay"
        ceremony, 120
Hostel Central, 75–76
Hotel Senorial, 45
Huaca, 42
Huacap, 37
Huacap Rimachi, 37
Huascaran, 29, 35
Huatuc, 37
Human sacrifice, 40–41
Humihua, 95, 99
Humming Bird God
    (Q'enti), 112
Hummingbird, nature
    spirit guide as, 64

I

Illa, 95, 97
Imagination, 185
Inca Cola, 12
Inca messenger (Ch'aska),
    15, 25, 162
Inca Trail, 12, 181–83, *See
    also* Archetypical
    Inca Trail
Inca Urcon, 33

Incan ceremonial tools,
    93–102
altar, 95
amethyst, 101
ara, 95, 98
bay leaves, 100
ceremonial candles, 96,
    101
chamomile, 100
chicken feather, 100
clay water vessel,
    100
cleansing, 94–95
coca leaves, 100
condor feather, 100
corn, 101
gathering, 93
hatumpi ccatu or
    despacho, 95, 97
humihua, 95, 99
illa, 95, 97
kuchuna ritual cloth,
    95–97
list of, 95–96
magic staff/wand, 95,
    99
magical/healing herbs,
    95, 99–100
Mama Ccocha, 95, 99
mismarumi, 95, 98
parrot feather, 100
pigeon feather, 100
potatoes, 101
purchasing, 94
quartz crystals, 101

Incan ceremonial tools,
    (*continued*)
reservoir athema, 95–96
  reservoir kuchuna,
    95–96
  ritual
    flute/whistle/zamp
    onas/pan pipes,
    100
  sage, 100
  salt, 95, 101
  selecting tools to start
    with, 94
  semiprecious
    gems/crystals, 96,
    101
  toucan feather, 100
  unkuna, 95, 97–98
  usable athema, 95–96
  usable kuchuna, 95–96
  vegetables, 96–97, 101
Incan creativity, 161–78
  Andean landscape art,
    171–73
  cultivating, 174–78
  dance, 167–69
  literature, 166–67
  music, 164–66
  pottery/ceramics,
    173–74
  weaving, 169–71
Incan dreams, 133–44
  Ayahuasca and San
    Pedro, 138–40

dreaming of a different
    reality, 136–38
  with a goal in mind,
    143–44
  overview of, 134–36
  as path to health, 137–38
  physical applications,
    141–43
  as powerful tool, 141–42
Incan Empire, 191
  Aclla, 38–39
  Amazon jungle, 30–31
  Ayllu, 38
  babies in, 38
  becoming a citizen of, 57
  charitable works of, 41
  coastline, 30
  darker aspects of, 41
  role of women in, 38–39
  rule of, 28
  and spiritual practices,
    68
  teenage boys in, 38
  and worship of
    Gods/Goddesses, 68
Incan Gods and
    Goddesses, 14–21
  alteration of form, 15
  assuming the energy of,
    109–10
  communication with, 14
  fighting Spanish
    conquistadors, in a
    dream, 20

first meeting with, 10
promise to, 9
requesting favors from,
    120–24
Incan life, 55–73
Incan painting, 174
Incan pantheon, 110–14
Incas:
adaptability of, 72–73
adaptation of Andean
    cultural advances,
    30
and astrology, 44
and astronomy, 44
attitude of, 180–81
culture of, 27, 28–29,
    79–80, 191
harsh life of, 39–40
history of, 27–44
laws of, 191
and matriarchal rule, 39
myths, 31–32
period of existence, 191
and prophecy, 44
reciprocity, importance
    of, 42
religious beliefs, 35–36
religious offices, 36–37
rites of passage, 81–82
rituals, 9, 67, 81–124
    author's first magical
        staff, 93–102
    background of,
        82–86

creating a reservoir
    for magical
    energies, 88–89
Incan ceremonial
    tools, 93–102
magical rituals, 87–88
proper energies, 103–6
Rites of Initiation,
    90–91
shamanic initiation
    rituals, 91–92
traditions of shamanic
    energies, passing
    down, 89
secrets of, 194
secrets of life, 191
secrets of time and
    space, 193
sixth sense/intuition,
    70
spirituality of, 38, 42–44
territory, 29–31
universal belief of, 37
use of term, 33
violations of law,
    punishment for,
    39–40
working with nature,
    191–92
written language, lack of,
    59
Inco Roca, 32
Initiation, 26
Inkarity, 111

Inti Rayman, 83–84
Inti (Sun God), 15, 22, 24,
    32, 34, 38, 42, 56, 91,
    111
Intip Chinan, 38
Intiwatana, 151

J

*Julia Cameron's Artistic
    Way Journal*, 176
Jungle shamans, 65

K

Kalasasaya, 157
Kallawayas, 150
Kettlehorn, Gene,
    183–84
K'intus, 121
Kuchuna ritual cloth,
    95–97
Kuntur (Condor
    Goddess), 112
Kuru (Corn Worm God),
    114

L

La Paz, 145, 151–54
Lake Titicaca region, 34,
    86, 145–46, 149
Land-bridge over the
    Bering Strait, 28

Langevin, Deborah, 1, 27,
    46, 46–53, 75, 77, 81,
    125–26, 130–31,
    153–54, 161, 168,
    189
Langevin, Henry, 1, 27,
    45–46, 77, 81,
    125–28, 149, 153,
    159, 161, 168, 189
    adoption of, 48–51
Langevin, Michael Peter,
    14, 17–18
Langevin, Sophia, 1, 27,
    45–46, 75, 77, 81,
    125–28, 153, 161,
    163, 168, 189
    adoption of, 49–51
Laziness, as a crime, 40
Lemuria, 156
Lightning God (Liviac),
    15, 23, 112
Lima, 11–12, 27, 45–46, 55,
    190–91
Lima airport, 189
Literature, 166–67
Liviac (Lightning God),
    15, 23, 112
Llama God
    (Guanocvicuna), 113
Llama Mama, 43
Llamas, 65, 68, 78, 171, 174
Lloque Yapanqui, 32
Llosa, Mario Vargas,
    166

Love, 183, 193
Luther, 127–29

M

Machota, 20, 27
Machu Picchu, 9, 12–14, 18,
    21, 22–23, 25, 30, 34,
    55, 123, 125, 172–73,
    181
  communication with
    Incan Gods and
    Goddesses at,
    14–15
  hiking to, 12–13, 14–15
Madonna of Copacabana,
    150
Magic staff/wand, 95, 99,
    102–3
Magical Blend magazine,
    46, 48, 77, 125
Magical energies, creating
    a reservoir for,
    88–89
Magical/healing herbs, 95,
    99–100
Magical rituals, 87–88
Mama Ccocha, 95, 99
Mama Hanka (Fertility
    Goddess), 113–14
Mama Occala, 162
Mama Occala (Goddess of
    the Oceans and
    Waters), 15, 112

Mama Ocollo, 32, 42, 60–61
Mama Quilla (Mother
    Goddess), 32, 34,
    111–12, 120
Mamak, 165
Manco Capa, 17, 32, 86
Matriarchal rule, and the
    Incas, 39
Mayta Capa Capac, 32
MB Media, 77
Medicine people, 140
Meditation, 110
  and finding your nature
    spirit guide, 63
Milky Way, 172
Mismarumi, 95, 98
Mocha, 29
Mohuseno, 165
Moon Goddess (Pacsa
    Mama), 15, 111–12,
    114–16
Mother Goddess (Mama
    Quilla), 32, 34,
    111–12, 120
Mountain Gods/Spirits
    (Apus), 42–43
Music, 164–66

N

Nariano, 12–14
Nasca culture, 29
Nature spirit guide,
    finding, 62–64

Nature spirits, power of, 64–65
Nawa, 31
Negative energies of deities, 110
Negative people, removing from our lives, 186
Night of the Holy Spirit, in Puno, 148–49
Nina Uilca, 39
Ninawillca, 121–22
Nuruda, Pablo, 167

O

Ocarina, 164
Offering of the essence, 118
Offerings, 122–23
Ollantaytambo, 173, 181
Oracle readers, 37

P

Paca Mama, 43
Paccarisca, 43
Pacco, 120–23
Pacha Mama (Earth Goddess), 15, 24–25, 43, 56, 60–61, 94, 101, 111, 123, 130, 133, 154, 193

Pachacuteq, 17–18, 29, 33–34, 36, 146, 181, 183
Pachatierra, 118
Pacsa Mama (Moon Goddess), 15, 42, 94, 111–12, 114–16
  invoking, 114–16
Painting, 174
Pan pipes, 165
  in ritual work, 100
Parasites, removing from our lives, 186
Parrot feather, 100
Partiri, 17–18, 23
  use of name, 17
Passion, 184
Pena, 153
Peru, 194
  adoption in, 48–50
  culture of, 12, 104–5
  decision to travel to, 10–11
  first journey to, 11–25
  higher vibration rising from, 190
  love of life in, 105–6
  as mystery personified, 176
  responsibility to, 14, 16
  as a world of dreams, 134
Peruvian creativity, 163–64
Phuyupatamarca, 173

Pigeon feather, 100
Pine trees, 68
Pinkuyllu, 165
Pinkuylluna mountain, 173
Pisac, 125–32, 172
    Incan graveyard, 128
    night on the town, 129–31
    Quechuen mass, 131–32
    ruins, 126–29
Plaza de Arms (Cusco), 78, 83
Plaza de Arms (Pisca), 127, 129–30
Plaza de Arms (Puno), 146
Porta Moldana, 55
Positive energies of deities, 110
Potatos, and the Incas, 29
Pottery, 173–74
    and the Incas, 29
Power spots, and rituals, 121
Practices, Inca people, 9
Prayers, 67, 110
Prayers to God and Jesus, 19
Pre-Christian shamans, 140
Priests, 37, 84
    initiation, 91

Principle of reciprocity, and Tiwanaku, 158
Proper energies, 103–6
Prophecy, and Incas, 44
Puma Orqo (Puma Goddess), 113
Puno, 145–49

Q

Q'enti (Humming Bird God), 112
Quality of life, 184
Quatro, 166
Quechuen, capacity for love and caring, 193–94
Quechuen language, 16, 17, 19, 66, 167
Quechuen mass, 131–32
Quechuen singing, 166
Queen Coya, 17
Quenua, 165
Quipus, 59–61, 141

R

Raquchi ruins (San Pedro), 146
Rattles, 165
Realigned vision, 60–62
Reality-altering, 84–85
Religious beliefs, 35–36
Reservoir athema, 95–96

Reservoir kuchuna,
    95–96
Riberyro, Julio Ramon, 167
Rites, 9
Rites of Initiation, 90–91
Rites of passage, 81–82
Ritual
    flute/whistle/zamp
        onas/pan pipes, 100
Rituals, 9, 67, 81–124
    author's first magical
        staff, 93–102
    background of, 82–86
    creating a reservoir for
        magical energies,
        88–89
    elements of, 83
    harvest rituals, 87
    Incan ceremonial tools,
        93–102
    Inti Rayman, 83–84
    of life, 84
    magical rituals, 87–88
    proper energies, 103–6
    purpose of, 83
    reality-altering, 84–85
    Rites of Initiation, 90–91
    shamanic initiation
        rituals, 91–92
    subject of, and modern
        Peru, 83
    and surrealism, 104
    traditions of shamanic
        energies, passing
        down, 89

Roman Catholic Church,
    84–85
and Ayllu beliefs, 43–44
and searches for
    treasure, 85

S

Sacred time, setting aside,
    58
Sacred Valley, 34, 125, 172,
    181
Sage, 100
Salt, in Incan ceremonial
    tools, 95, 101
Samincha, 118
San Padro Calcus,
    91–92
San Pedro, 146
Sapa Incas, 28–29, 32–35,
    36, 39, 41, 84, 90–91,
    171
    defined, 32
Sara Mama (Corn
    Goddess), 43
Self-examination, 58–60
Semiprecious
    gems/crystals, in
        Incan ceremonial
        tools, 96, 101
Serpent's Tooth, 23
Shalshas, 165
Shamanic energies,
    passing down
        traditions of, 89

Shamanic initiation
    rituals, 91–92
Shamanic wisdom,
    92
Shamans, 68, 71, 83–84, 84,
    120
Shamans of the Amazon,
    65
Shape shifting, 65
Sheep, 78, 171
Shining Path rebels,
    129–30, 142
Siku, 164
Sillustan Atuncolla,
    147–48
Sinchi Roca, 32
Singing, 19
Sisuani, 146
Soothsayers, 37
Spanish conquistadors,
    fighting, in a dream,
    20–21
Spirits of the four
    quadrants, 88
Spriitual Incas, astral
    travels of, 87
Striber, Whitley, 155
Substance abuse, compared
    to activities we love,
    186–87
Sun God (Inti), 15, 22, 24,
    32, 34, 38, 42, 56, 91,
    111
Sun Temple (Cusco),
    85–86

T

Tacna, 179
Tathuantinsuyo, 33
Temple of the Moon, 55,
    123, 150
Temple of the Stones
    Standing Up
    (Kalasasaya),
    157
Temple of the Sun, 36,
    150
Tewunaku culture, 29
Textiles, 169–71
Thunder God (Chuqui
    Yllayllapa), 15, 23,
    112
Tiwanaku, 31, 155–59
    as center of ancient
        wisdom/science,
        158–59
    political organization,
        158
    and principle of
        reciprocity, 158
    pyramids at, 156–57
    Solar door, 157
Tomboohiebiaz, 165
Topa Inca, 34
Torenez, Tom, 138–40
Toucan feather, 100
Tree of Life, 173
Tupac Amaru, 20–21
Tupac Yupanqui, 32
Turtle Cafe, 11

U

Uilca, 37
Uillac Uma, 36–37, 39
Umaylo peninsula, 148
University of Lima, and
    searches for
    treasure, 85
Unkuna, 95, 97–98
Uros floating islands, 145,
    147
Uros language, 147
Urubamba River, 172
Urubamba River valley,
    128
Usable athema, 95–96
Usable kuchuna, 95–96

V

Vallejo, Cesar, 167
Valley of the Moon, 152
Van Daniken, Erich, 155
Vegetables, in Incan
    ceremonial tools,
    96–97, 101
Vicuna, 171
Vilcabamba, 86
Violations of law,
    punishment, 39–40
Violins, 166
Vira, 111
Virgins of the Sun, 38, 141
    initiation, 91

Vision, 185
    realignment of, 60–62
Visions of
    death/destruction,
    22–23
Visualization, 67, 76–77

W

Wak'rapuku, 165
Wari culture, 29
Warrior God (Chaven),
    113
Water Goddess (Mama
    Occala), 15
Wawas, 38
Wayna Capa, 34–35
Wayna Picchu, 14, 16, 21,
    173
Weaving, 169–71
Weavings, and the Incas,
    29
Weeping Goddess
    (Chavene), 113
Wells, Betty, 75, 123
Wells, Joaquin, 75
Wells, Mila, 75
Wells, Tim, 75
Whistle, in ritual work,
    100
Willcamayu River, 172
Winay Wayna, 12, 15
Wind instruments,
    164–65

Wiracocha, 146
Wiracocha (Creator God),
   15, 18, 24, 31–32, 33,
   111, 173
Wise women, 140
Work, 185
Writing Down the Bones
   (Goldberg), 176

Y

Yahuar Huacac, 32
Yuquanqui, 33

Z

Zamponas, 153, 164
   in ritual work, 100